get
your
life
back

EVERYDAY PRACTICES
FOR A WORLD GONE MAD

STUDY GUIDE I SIX SESSIONS

JOHN ELDREDGE

NELSON
BOOKS

An Imprint of Thomas Nelson

Published in Nashville, Tennessee, by Nelson Books. Nelson Books is a registered trademark of HarperCollins Christian Publishing, Inc.

Published in association with Yates & Yates, LLP, www.yates2.com.

All Scripture quotations, unless otherwise noted, are taken from the Holy Bible, New International Version®. NIV ®. Copyright 1973, 1978, 1994, 2011 by Biblica, Inc.®. Used by permission. All rights reserved worldwide.

Scripture quotations marked MSG [or The Message] are taken from *The Message.* Copyright © by Eugene H. Peterson 1993, 1994, 1995, 1996, 2000, 2001, 2002. Used by permission of NavPress. All rights reserved. Represented by Tyndale House Publishers, Inc.

Scripture quotations marked NLT are taken from the Holy Bible, New Living Translation. © 1996, 2004, 2007, 2013, 2015 by Tyndale House Foundation. Used by permission of Tyndale House Publishers, Inc., Carol Stream, Illinois 60188. All rights reserved.

Thomas Nelson titles may be purchased in bulk for educational, business, fundraising, or sales promotional use. For information, please e-mail SpecialMarkets@ThomasNelson.com.

ISBN 978-0-310-09702-0 (softcover)
ISBN 978-0-310-09710-5 (ebook)

First Printing January 2020 / Printed in the United States of America

CONTENTS

INTRODUCTION

There's a madness to our moment, and we need to name it for the lunacy it is. Because it's taking our lives hostage.

First, there's the blistering pace of life. Everyone I talk to says they feel busier than ever. Then there's the deluge of media coming at us in a sort of mesmerizing digital spell. This is all very hard on the soul. But what got my attention was what was happening to me *as a person*.

I found myself flinching when a friend texted and asked for some time. I didn't want to open email for fear of the demands I'd find there. I had a shorter and shorter fuse in traffic. I felt numb to tragic news reports. It made me wonder—*am I becoming a less loving person?* I had little capacity for relationships and the things that bring me life—a walk in the woods, dinner with friends, a cold plunge in a mountain lake. When I did steal a moment for something life-giving, I was so distracted I couldn't enjoy it.

Then I realized—it wasn't a failure of love or compassion. These were symptoms of a soul pushed too hard, strung out, haggard, fried. My soul just can't do life at the speed of smart-phones. But I was asking it to; everybody's asking theirs to.

I'm guessing you've experienced something similar. It's likely why you've picked up this study—your soul is looking for something. Are you aware of what it is?

If we had more of God, that would really help. We could draw upon his love and strength, his wisdom and resilience. After all, God is the fountain of life (Psalm 36:9). If we had more of his lavish life bubbling up in us, it would be a rescue in this soul-scorching hour.

Jesus heard even my surface prayers; he came to my rescue and began to lead me into a number of helps and practices, what I would call graces. Simple things, like a One Minute Pause, that were accessible and surprising in their power to restore. Learning "Benevolent Detachment"—the ability to let things go. Allowing for some transition in my day, instead of just blasting from one thing to the next. Drinking in the beauty God was providing in quiet moments. My soul began to recover, feel better, do better. I began to enjoy my life with God so much more. I began to get my life back.

This study guide is a companion to the book *Get Your Life Back*. You can do this series as part of a group—or on your own. Either way, you'll want to have a copy of the book and video. You'll note that the book has fourteen chapters and this is a six-session study guide. Several sessions combine two chapters; others focus on one. Some chapters of the book are not included due to space. That's why we highly recommend reading the book in full in addition to being part of this study.

If you're leading a group, a guide has been provided for you in the back of this study. Each session in this guide has these distinct offerings:

- Welcome / Introduction
- "Getting Started" Questions
- Scripture Reading
- Video Summary
- Group Session Questions
- Closing Prayer Topics
- Giving It a Try—Personal Practice / Exercise
- Between-Sessions Personal Study (Five Days)
- Recommended Reading for Next Session

God *wants* to come to us and restore our lives. He really does. But the process needs to be accessible and sustainable. We've all tried exercise, diets, Bible study programs that began with vim and verve but over time got shoved to the side, lost in the chaos. I have a gym membership; I rarely use it. There are those books I haven't finished, loads of podcasts too. Rest assured—the graces I am offering here are within reach of a normal life. I think you'll find them simple, sustainable, and refreshing.

God wants to strengthen and renew your soul; Jesus longs to give you more of himself. "Are you tired? Worn out? Burned out on religion? Come to me. Get away with me and you'll recover your life . . . and you'll learn to live freely and lightly" (Matthew 11:28–30, MSG). You can get your life back; you can live freely and lightly. The world may be harsh, but God is gentle; he knows what your life is like.

What we need to do is put ourselves in places that allow us to receive his help. This six-week study will show you how.

SESSION 1

THE ONE MINUTE PAUSE

"I have calmed and quieted myself."

DAVID, PSALM 131:2

WELCOME

I wonder how many people in your office, your gym, your daily commute could say they've cultivated a quiet heart? What we assume is a normal lifestyle is absolute insanity to the God-given nature of our heart and soul.

Nonetheless, this is the world we live in, raise our kids in, navigate our careers in, and so we need to find things that are simple and accessible to begin to take back our souls.

My premise is simple. The world is nuts. It's gone off the rails and is trying to take our hearts and souls with it. If you're doing this study in a group, I bet you barely made it here. If you're watching this by yourself, you're likely squeezing it into some narrow window of margin. Everyone I know, all my friends, are so busy these days.

Part of the problem is we're trying to keep up with the pace of technology. We're asking our souls to live at the speed of the smartphone and the laptop and it can't be done. It's brutal. So there's the pace of life, right?

And then there is this tsunami of information coming at us. We're spending four hours a day on our mobile devices, three hours using apps of various kinds, ten hours a day consuming media of some sort. That's more information in one week than would crash a laptop. Right? And it's not just information. It's scandal and chaos and politics and gossip and the trauma of the world. This is hard on the soul. There's very little room left to be human anymore.

My musician friends tell me that they're not playing much music these days, and my gardening friends didn't have a chance to plant this year what they wanted to plant. We're all just living right at the edge of our margin.

Most of us get home on most days in a state of exhaustion, numb on our good days, fried more often than we'd like to admit. It's like what Bilbo said: "We feel thin and stretched like butter, scraped over too much, bread."[1]

That's why I wrote this series. So we can get our lives back. Jesus has a way out. Jesus can show you the escape hatch to this madness that we're living in. He began to show me the way out through a number of simple daily practices that helped me breathe again and restore my soul. He will do the same for you.

GETTING STARTED

If you or any of your group members are just getting to know one another, take a few minutes to introduce yourselves. Then, to kick things off, discuss one of the following questions:

1. Are you happy and carefree most of the time? Why or why not?
2. Would you describe yourself as rested and refreshed? Why or why not?
3. Do you look forward to your future? Why or why not?

CORE SCRIPTURE

Invite someone to read aloud the following passage. Listen for fresh insight and share any new thoughts with the group through the questions that follow.

> *Are you tired? Worn out? Burned out on religion? Come to me. Get away with me and you'll recover your life . . . and you'll learn to live freely and lightly.*
> —MATTHEW 11:28–30, MSG

1. What is Jesus' general assumption about us within his three questions? How accurately does this describe you?

2. What is his core invitation?

3. What are the results dependent on?

VIDEO TEACHING

Play the video segment for session 1. A summary of the key points is provided for your benefit as well as space to take additional notes.

Summary

- We tend to go through our days with no margin—racing from one thing to the next. As the pace win which we're living accelerates, we don't seem to have even one minute to just pause, breathe, and release it all to Jesus.

- The big lie is how technology was supposed to create room in our lives for all those things that we enjoy. It's done the exact opposite, increasing our workload as we try to keep up to the pace of a world gone completely mad.

- On average, we spend four hours a day on our mobile devices, three hours using apps of various kinds, and ten hours a day consuming media of some sort.

- It's not just the tsunami of information that is coming at us but also the trauma of the world. It's hard on the soul. There's very little room left to be human anymore.

- The One Minute Pause is the practice of taking sixty seconds to simply breathe, be quiet, and let your soul catch up to you. This isn't a time to pray, process, or be productive—but simply to breathe.

- Benevolent Detachment is the practice of releasing everyone and everything to God. "Benevolent" because it's not angry or cynical but done in love and kindness. "Detachment" because it's a recognition we can't carry the world. We are not God.

- Jesus is actually really serious about us turning things over to him on a regular basis (Matthew 11:28-30). The One Minute Pause and Benevolent Detachment are two great ways to do so.

Notes

GROUP DISCUSSION

Take a few minutes to go through the following questions with your group.

1. In what specific ways has the pace of your life accelerated in the past few years?

2. Are there certain things you've had to give up recently— such as hobbies or simple pleasures—just to keep up?

3. Were you surprised to hear we spend ten hours a day consuming media of some sort? What has the effect of this been on your soul?

4. What was the experience of the One Minute Pause like for you? Was it difficult to not try to be productive during that time—or easy to simply let your soul breathe?

5. What does 1 Peter 5 say we should do with our worries and cares? How good are you at practicing this?

6. Benevolent Detachment involves learning to release everyone and everything to God. What are the hardest things for you to release to God? Why?

CLOSING PRAYER

Wrap up your time together with prayer. Remember, prayer is simply talking to God. Here are a few ideas of what you could pray about based on the topics of this first session:

- Ask God to reveal the ways that you are running on empty—physically and spiritually.
- Pray for God to help you learn how to live freely and lightly.
- Commit to doing the One Minute Pause each day.
- Cast all your cares and burdens to God and leave them there.
- Release everyone and everything to the Father through Benevolent Detachment.

GIVING IT A TRY

Your first weekly practice involves the One Minute Pause. It can be used in many ways: for prayer or silence, to find your heart again, or to enjoy a moment of beauty. We'll develop this practice throughout this study.

To get started:

- Pick one or two moments each day when you are least likely to be interrupted.
- Set your phone alarm to remind you. Pick a notification sound that is gracious, not adrenaline producing ("Bell," or better "Silk." Not "Suspense" or "News Flash" for you iPhone users). You are not

sounding an alarm; you are inviting your soul to a gracious pause.

In these sixty seconds:

- Be still and simply breathe.
- Let everyone and everything go.
- Ask for more of God: Jesus—I need more of you; fill me with more of you, God. Restore our union; fill me with your life.

I have developed an app to help you practice the One Minute Pause; it's beautiful, and I think it will be of great service to you. You can find it for free in the app store.

This one simple practice will open the door to many others. Your soul is going to thank you.

SESSION 1

BETWEEN-SESSIONS PERSONAL STUDY

I n this section, you can further explore the material we've covered this week. If you haven't already done so, we encourage you to read chapter 1, "The One Minute Pause," and chapter 2, "Benevolent Detachment," of *Get Your Life Back* at this time. Each day offers a short reading from the book—along with reflection questions designed to take you deeper into the themes of this week's study. Journal or just jot a few thoughts after each question. At the start of the next session, there will be a few minutes to share any insights . . . but the primary goal of these questions is for your personal growth and private reflection.

DAY ONE: FIGHT OR FLIGHT

We live in a world that triggers our souls into vigilance far too often. The complexity of modern life is mind-boggling: the constantly changing social terrain of what's appropriate, the level of trauma we navigate in people's lives. The typical sounds of a city trigger adrenaline responses in us all day long; that deep throbbing bass *whump* coming from the car four lanes over, the one you feel all through your body, is not that different from the sound of distant artillery. Thanks to the smartphone and the web, you are confronted on a daily basis with more information than any previous generation had to deal with! And it's not just information; it's the suffering of the entire planet, in minute detail, served up on your feed daily. Add to this the pace at which most of us are required to live our lives.

This morning I can't tell whether my soul is more in fight or flight. But I do know this—I don't like the state I'm in. I didn't sleep well last night (one of the many consequences of living in a hyper-charged world), and after I finally conked out, I overslept, woke up late, and ever since I've felt behind on everything.

I rushed through breakfast, dashed out the door to get to some meetings, and now I'm rattled. I don't like that feeling, and I don't like the consequences. When I'm rattled, I'm easily irritated with people. I didn't have the patience to listen to what my wife was trying to say this morning. I find it hard to hear from God, and I don't like feeling untethered from him.

I notice now in my rattled state that I want to eat something fatty and sugary; I want something that's going to make me feel better *now*. When we're unsettled, unnerved, unhinged, it's human nature to seek a sense of equilibrium, stability, and I find myself wondering—how many addictions begin here, with just wanting a little comfort? Get out of the rattled place and soothe ourselves with "a little something"?

We live in a crazy-making world. So much stimulation rushes at us with such unrelenting fury, we are overstimulated most of the time. Things that nourish us—a lingering conversation, a leisurely stroll through the park, time to savor both making and then enjoying dinner—these are being lost at an alarming rate; we simply don't have room for them. Honestly, I think most people live their daily lives along a spectrum from slightly rattled to completely fried as their normal state of being.

In the late morning, I finally do what I should have from the beginning—I pause, get quiet, settle down. I give myself permission to simply pause, a little breathing room to come back to myself and God. My breathing returns to normal (I didn't even notice I was holding my breath). A little bit of space begins to clear around me. Suddenly, somewhere outside, someone has just fired up a leaf blower—one of the great pariahs of the human race, the enemy of all tranquility. My body tenses, the stress returns, and because I'm paying attention, I see for myself how the constant stimulation of our chaotic world causes us to live in a state of hypervigilance.

Notice—are your muscles relaxed right now or tense? Is your breathing deep and relaxed, or are you taking short, shallow breaths? Are you able to read this leisurely, or do you feel you need to get through it quickly? Most of the day we simply plow through a myriad of diverse tasks, checking boxes, "getting stuff done." It frazzles the soul, so we look to all our "comforters" to calm down. But I know my salvation is not in the Frappuccino nor the fudge.

1. Does your soul feel like it's in fight or flight mode now? What are the signs that help you know this?

2. When you're in a rattled state, what do you look to for temporary relief or a little comfort? How helpful has that been in the long term?

3. When was the last time you gave yourself permission to simply pause? Given how helpful it is, why does this seem so unattainable most days?

DAY TWO: THE ONE MINUTE PAUSE

A practice that's become an absolute lifesaver is the One Minute Pause. I simply take sixty seconds to be still and let everything go.

As I enter the pause, I begin with release. I let it all go—the meetings, what I know is coming next, the fact I'm totally behind on everything, all of it. I simply let it go. I pray, *Jesus—I give everyone and everything to you.* I keep repeating it until I feel like I'm actually releasing and detaching. *I give everyone and everything to you, God.* All I'm trying to accomplish right now is a little bit of soul-space. I'm not trying to fix anything or figure anything out. I'm not trying to release everything perfectly or permanently. That takes a level of maturity most of us haven't found. But I can let it go for sixty seconds. (That's the brilliance of the pause—all we are asking ourselves to do is let go for sixty seconds.) And as I do, even as I say it out loud—*I give everyone and everything to you*—my soul cooperates a good bit. I'm settling down.

I even sigh, that good sigh.

Then I ask for more of God: *Jesus—I need more of you; fill me with more of you, God. Restore our union; fill me with your life.*

You'll be surprised what a minute can do for you. Even more so as you get practiced at it. Honestly, you can do this pause nearly anytime, anywhere—in your car, on the train, after you get off your phone. I know it seems small, but we have to start somewhere. This pause is accessible; it's doable.

The desert fathers of the third and fourth century were a courageous, ragtag group, followers of Jesus who fled the madness of their world to seek a life of beauty and simplicity with God in the silent desert. For they saw the world as "a shipwreck from which every man has to swim for their life."[2] And think of it: they had no cell phones, no internet, no media per se, not one automobile, Starbucks, or leaf blower. The news that came their way was local; they did not carry the burdens of every community in the world. They walked everywhere they went. Therefore, they lived at the pace of *three miles an hour* (!). Yet they felt the world sucking the life out of them, and they decided to do something about it.

And so we who live in a far more insane hour and who want to find a better life in God ought to be the first to adopt a few practices that get us out of the madness and into a more settled way of living. Most of us would be happy simply to be a little less rattled.

1. How was your first attempt at the One Minute Pause? Where did your thoughts go? How long did the minute seem to last?

2. Part of the One Minute Pause is asking for more of Jesus and to be filled with his life. Is this request of greater union with God something you've asked for before? How do you think that might help the state of your soul to do so regularly?

3. The desert fathers described this world as "a shipwreck from which every man has to swim for their life." Would you agree or disagree? Why?

DAY THREE: FREEDOM OF HEART

I'm sitting on a bluff in the wild southwest corner of Wyoming, sweeping the horizon with my binoculars. The view up here is staggering—only sagebrush and coarse grasses for hundreds of miles in every direction; I can see the curve of the earth. It's going to be a hot August day. Heat waves are already shimmering in my view, making it hard to spot my quarry. Most folks would probably call these the badlands. Blistering in summer, freezing all winter, nearly always windy—but I come here because wild horses love this country. They feel safe out here.

There are still hundreds of herds of wild horses running through the American West, a fact that makes my soul happy. Wildness, open spaces, and animals living in utter freedom are all good for our humanity. Sometimes we need geography to usher our soul into spaciousness, lightheartedness. And so I've come.

A golden eagle is sitting only twenty yards downslope in front of me. Golden eagles are massive raptors, with seven-foot wingspans and the strength to carry off fawns and lambs. This one is perched on the edge of a cliff, scanning the alkaline landscape for prey. It's a perfect perch for him; with the updrafts coming up the bluff, all he has to do is spread his wings, step off, and he's gone. I can't believe he hasn't seen me. Maybe he has and simply doesn't care. I sigh with peace and happiness.

At dawn this morning I got in my truck, pointed myself north, and just . . . drove away. For a blissful week of solitude. No real plans: only my camping gear, fishing rod, and maps of the Wind River range, Yellowstone, and Montana. This is an unplanned, last-minute trip—something Jesus practically insisted on. Many moons have come and gone since I took time to get away, care for my soul, find God.

And I must tell you, it's an extraordinary feeling to have your world fading in the rearview mirror, nothing but an open road before you.

It's a practice Jesus himself cherished (minus the truck). I've always been intrigued by his ability to just up and walk away from his world. Right there in the opening chapter of Mark, with excitement building and crowds swelling all round him, Jesus disappears. He just . . . leaves.

Very early in the morning, while it was still dark, Jesus got up, left the house and went off to a solitary place, where he prayed. Simon and his companions went to look for him, and when they found him, they exclaimed: "Everyone is looking for you!" Jesus replied, "Let us go somewhere else" (Mark 1:35–38).

Jesus models a freedom of heart I think every one of us would love to have. His ability to disengage himself from his world is so alluring.

So, like a good disciple, I've done the same. Everyone is wanting something from me, so I've followed my Master and . . . left. If I wanted to see wild horses I probably should have gotten here sooner, but ever since I left home this morning, I've been moseying, stopping to read those "points of historical interest" I usually blast by. It'll take a few days to enter in, but already I can feel that exquisite condition coming on—a rare, carefree lightheartedness.

1. How does Jesus model purposeful soul care for us?

2. What would it feel like for you to find moments to leave the madness of your world for time with God?

3. When is the last time you've felt the "rare, carefree lightness" described in today's reading? What does it do for your heart to know not only is this available but it is also God's desire for you?

DAY FOUR: BENEVOLENT DETACHMENT

We are talking in this study about making room in our lives for God so that we might receive more of his wonderful self in us and, with that, the vibrancy and resiliency we crave as human beings. There are external ways we can do this, simple steps like the One Minute Pause. And there are internal ways we do this as well.

To make room for God to fill the vessel of our soul, we have to begin moving out some of the unnecessary clutter that continually accumulates there like the junk drawer in your kitchen. Everybody has a junk drawer, that black hole for car keys, pens, paper clips, gum, all the small flotsam and jetsam that accumulates over time. Our souls accumulate stuff, too, pulling it in like a magnet. And so Augustine said we must empty ourselves of all that fills us so that we may be filled with what we are empty of.[3] Over time I've found no better practice to help clear out my cluttered soul than the practice of Benevolent Detachment. The ability to let it go, walk away—not so much physically but emotionally, *soulfully*.

Allow me to explain. We are aiming for release, turning over into the hands of God whatever is burdening us *and leaving it there*. It's so easy to get caught up in the drama in unhealthy ways, and then we are unable to see clearly, set boundaries, respond freely.

Mature adults have learned how to create healthy distance between themselves and the thing they have become entangled with. Thus the word *detachment*. It means getting untangled, stepping out of the quagmire; it means peeling apart the Velcro by which this person, relationship, crisis, or global issue has attached itself to you. Or you to it. Detachment means getting some healthy distance. Social media overloads our empathy. So I use the word "benevolent" in referring to this necessary kind of detachment because we're not talking about cynicism or resignation. Benevolent means kindness. It means something done in love. Jesus invites us into a way of living where we are genuinely comfortable turning things over to him:

> Then Jesus said, "Come to me, all of you who are weary and carry heavy burdens, and I will give you rest. Take my yoke upon you. Let me teach you, because I am humble and gentle at heart, and you will find rest for your souls. For my yoke is easy to bear, and the burden I give you is light" (Matthew 11:28–30, NLT).

Are you tired? Worn out? Burned out on religion? Come to me. Get away with me and you'll recover your life. I'll show you how to take a real rest. Walk with me and work with me—watch how I do it. Learn the unforced rhythms of grace. I won't lay anything heavy or ill-fitting on you. Keep company with me and you'll learn to live freely and lightly (Matthew 11:28–30, MSG).

Millions of people are feeling massively overburdened and looking for some way to lighten their heavy emotional load. This is something Jesus is particularly good at helping us with, which is why learning Benevolent Detachment is such a timely grace.

1. To make room for God to fill the vessel of our souls, we have to begin moving out some of the unnecessary clutter that continually accumulates there like the junk drawer in your kitchen. What specific things do you need to clear from your cluttered soul?

2. Describe what Benevolent Detachment is by writing a few thoughts on the meaning of each word. How might turning things over to God in this way help you lighten your load?

3. What most stood out to you from the words in Matthew 11:28–30? Why?

DAY FIVE: GIVE EVERYONE AND EVERYTHING TO ME

Worry is only one of a hundred things that burden our souls. Genuine concern is just as dangerous, maybe more so because it's grounded in something noble—your concerns for your aging parents, a sick friend, a people group, a cause crying out for justice. A friend of mine runs a home rescuing trafficked girls. He wrote last week to say that the government facility is overcrowded, and they asked him if he could take eleven girls. The heartbreak was my friend had room for only five; he had to make the brutal call. Today a therapist colleague who does remarkable work with military men and women suffering PTSD lamented he can't see enough people. "We're losing too many to suicide," he said. "It tears me up I can't help more."

Those kinds of things can fill a backpack and make it mighty heavy.

Jesus began teaching me about Benevolent Detachment almost two years ago. Every time I would turn to him with a question, he would say, *Give everyone and everything to me.* The invitation rang so true; I knew I needed to learn this. So I began to practice it as best I could. But then Jesus kept repeating the invitation. I'd be asking about something entirely unrelated to the people in my life—car repairs, scheduling a trip, my tax returns—and Jesus would reply, *Give everyone and everything to me.* It was irritating. I finally realized that the reason he kept repeating it was because I wasn't practicing it very well. I was carrying people. Worrying about things.

We are far more entangled with the world than we know. And the thing is, people and causes have a way of entangling themselves with *you* too.

Some of this has to do with the moment we live in and the obliteration of social boundaries.

Thanks to social media, everyone's life is open and accessible through Facebook, Twitter, Instagram—all of it. We've created an assumption that you can enter and observe, or engage, with anyone, anywhere, anytime. There are no boundaries. We've created an assumption that we're entitled to enter anyone else's private space at any time. It's very harmful. Cell phones have been a major contributor to this loss of personal space. A friend who is a successful businessman explained to me how the rules of corporate loyalty have changed: "They expect you to be available anytime, day or night, because of this," he said, holding up his phone. "They can text you, call you 24/7. You are now considered to be available anytime, all the time. Those are the new rules."

I told myself as I drove off into the wilderness this morning that I would turn my phone off for a few days to enforce my disengagement. But I've checked my messages several times in the last hour. It's so odd to be dialed into the technology of the world while I drive through rural countryside. This was the world of my grandmother, raised her entire life in rural America. Back in the day if you wanted to have a conversation with someone, if you wanted to enter their world, you literally had to enter their world. You got in your car and drove to their farm and sat on their porch and had a conversation. You also understood that there are appropriate hours for doing so. People were very aware that there were public moments and private moments, public spaces and private spaces.

All that is completely gone now.

There is this unspoken assumption that anyone can enter your world anytime. It's suffocating to the soul; there's no breathing room. People are looking for some way to push this stuff back just a few feet. Gimme some space for heaven's sake.

Exactly.

Benevolent Detachment is your way out.

1. What does the invitation to release everyone and everything to Jesus provoke in you? Why?

2. How has the expectation from social media that you be available everywhere at all times affected the rhythm of your day and your ability to rest or simply breathe?

3. Who do you need to release to God now? What projects or deadlines do you need to release? Be specific . . . and then release them as you write your responses below.

RECOMMENDED READING

Before your group meets for the next session, we encourage you to read chapter 4, "Simple Unplugging," of *Get Your Life Back*. That chapter will be the focus of session 2.

SESSION 2

SIMPLE UNPLUGGING

"As our mental lives become more fragmented, what is at stake often seems to be nothing less than the question of whether one can maintain a coherent self."

MATTHEW CRAWFORD,
THE WORLD BEYOND YOUR HEAD

WELCOME

'm sitting at my desk this morning, writing. My phone, lying face-down next to me, vibrates. Because yes, I did silence it, but I didn't turn it off. The vibration notification causes a reflex response in me, a learned response. I pick it up, read the text that just came in, reply, set it down, and turn back to my work. But it takes me a few moments to recover my train of thought. Meanwhile, I remember that a friend sent me a link to an article that applies to what I'm writing this morning, so I decide to have a look now that I'm no longer engaged in the actual act of writing. The article is helpful and does get my thoughts rolling again, but as you know, when you get to any news website you don't simply receive the article. You're confronted with a visual experience that is one third article and two thirds advertising—and which of those is typically more arresting?

I get five seconds into the article when a pop-up screen requests my email address.

This stuff is so irritating.

I switch screens (for, of course, I have multiple screens open in the background, as most desktop and mobile users do) to one of those helpful online Bible programs so I can look up a verse. Quicker than I can type "Psalm 1," Google ads pop up in banners and columns on the right and left side of the screen. Google knows my buying habits—Google actually knows a freaky amount of information about me and you—and suddenly here are all sorts of ads perfectly tailored to get my attention. The hunting pack I was looking at for my son's birthday, the exact earrings I bought my wife and four others like them. There are videos and moving banners, and they are *so* distracting.

I realize now I'm totally removed from writing, so I choose to settle back into the presence of Christ with some worship. I was listening to something on YouTube earlier, so that screen is open in the background too. But of course the worship does not play first; first comes the movie trailer, car promotion, something marketing geniuses spent millions on because they know they have five seconds before I get to click Skip Ad.

Finally, like a man who has run the gauntlet, I am able to return to my work. Then another notification on my phone: my weather app is alerting me of possible snow flurries this evening, and while I pick it up to turn the thing off entirely, a video pops up of some bizarre sea creature washed up on the beaches of Florida, "never before seen by man!"

This is our daily. This is the stuff that comes at us all the time.

It's like driving at night into a snowstorm, your headlights illuminating the flurries racing at your windshield. It's all you can see. No wonder so few people enjoy the graces of beauty or practice Benevolent Detachment. Or even find it possible to take a moment's pause. Our attention is constantly being taken hostage.

But we can take it back.

GETTING STARTED

If you or any of your group members are just getting to know one another, take a few minutes to introduce yourselves. Then, to kick things off, discuss one of the following questions:

1. How hard would it be to cut your social media use in half for a week? How much time would you get back based on your current weekly time on social media?
2. What would you miss the most? Why?
3. How might you use this "found" time for more soul care?

CORE SCRIPTURE

Invite someone to read aloud the following passage from Psalm 119. Listen for fresh insight and share any new thoughts with the group through the questions that follow.

> Oh, how I love your law!
>   I meditate on it all day long.
> Your commands are always with me
>   and make me wiser than my enemies.
> I have more insight than all my teachers,
>   for I meditate on your statutes.

—PSALM 119:97–99

1. Did the psalmist feel like spending time with God was a duty or a joy?

2. Was giving God his attention a priority for him? How do you know?

3. What two tangible benefits came from this approach? Would those be helpful in your world?

VIDEO TEACHING

Watch the video segment for session 2. A summary is provided for your benefit as well as space to take additional notes.

Summary

- To create soul space and find more room for God in our lives, we're going to have to deal with our consumption of—and attachment to—technology.

- According to author Nicholas Carr, our use of media—particularly the internet, our mobile devices, and social media—is literally changing the way we think and process.

- This isn't simply a cultural crisis but a spiritual crisis. The soul's need for love, restoration, and connection with God hinges on our ability to give God our attention.

- Research shows a direct correlation between our amount and consumption of social media and the rise of anxiety and depression in our culture.

- No human soul was made to ever endure all the sorrows and heartache of the entire planet delivered daily on our mobile devices.

- The desert fathers were a beautiful, holy, ragtag group of believers in the early centuries of the church that went away from society in order to try and find a soulful life again and recover from the toxicity of their world. It's time for a new era of desert fathers and mothers—those willing to be counter-cultural and not live attached to the daily chaos.

- We are meant to be filled with the life and the love of God, but we face a double bind. In the very moment we need strong and resilient souls to resist that madness of this world, that same madness is taking our attention away from the very graces we need to thrive.

Notes

GROUP DISCUSSION

Take a few minutes to go through the following questions
with your group.

1. What affect has the practice of the One Minute Pause
   had on your heart this past week? Is it becoming more
   natural the more you do it?

2. Would you say you're drawn to—or perhaps addicted to—
   the things that offer distraction? Why or why not?

3. Studies show how we consume information literally
   changes the way we think and process it. Has this been
   the case for you? If so, how?

4. What technology would you least want to give up? Most days, do you feel it serves you or you end up serving it? Would those close to you agree?

5. While in a meeting or in-person conversation, how hard is it for you to ignore your phone for a few minutes when it chirps or it beeps? Assuming that you aren't expecting an urgent call, what do you think drives the need to always be reachable?

6. So much of our world can be experienced digitally. In what ways do you seek out "real" things—like chopping vegetables, doing a puzzle, going for a walk, or playing an instrument? What benefit might those things bring?

CLOSING PRAYER

Wrap up your time together with prayer. Remember, prayer is simply talking to God. Here are a few ideas of what you could pray about based on the topics of this second session:

- Pray that God would help you be more fully present to the people in your life.
- Ask for the strength and desire to unplug from the distraction of technology .
- Commit to continue making time for the One Minute Pause each day.
- Release everyone and everything to the Father through Benevolent Detachment.
- Mediate regularly on the beauty and goodness of God.

GIVING IT A TRY

Our phones are perhaps the hardest things to unplug from. It's almost always with us—and we have countless reasons why we can't be without it.

That's why this week's practice involves your phone. The invitation is to unplug more so you can be more present . . . and whole. If you create a little bit of sacred space every day, God will meet you there. And you will begin to love it.

The challenge is to do *all four* practices for seven days:

- Turn your phone off at 8:00 PM. Give yourself some evening time for real things.

- Banish all technology from your bedroom.
- Don't check your phone as soon as you wake up in the morning. Give your soul mercy to wake up, enjoy a few peaceful moments.
- When your phone chirps or vibrates, don't react. Make it wait till you pick it up.

During the week, notice which of the above was the hardest. Pay attention to when you most want to reach for the phone—either for distraction or comfort. You may want to discuss how it went with the group during the next session.

These four simple practices will help to make your phone a tool again, something that serves you instead of the other way around.

BETWEEN-SESSIONS PERSONAL STUDY

In this section, you can further explore the material we've covered this week. If you haven't already done so, we encourage you to read chapter 4, "Simple Unplugging," of *Get Your Life Back* at this time. Each day offers a short reading from the book—along with reflection questions designed to take you deeper into the themes of this week's study. Journal or just jot a few thoughts after each question. At the start of the next session, there will be a few minutes to share any insights . . . but the primary goal of these questions is for your personal growth and private reflection.

DAY ONE: THE ASSAULT ON YOUR ATTENTION

There is an insistent, unrelenting assault on our *attention*.

News. Marketing. Notifications. Alerts. Status updates. Postings. An incessant barrage of "information" competing for our attention. You can't get away from it. I fly a bit for my living, and airlines know you are a captive audience. Before takeoff, but once I'm buckled in my seat, ads begin to play on the screen before me, and I can't turn them off. Walk through a modern airport—it's a shopping mall designed like a casino, hard to find your way out. I leave the airport and jump in a cab; a screen facing me immediately starts playing commercials, loudly. Driving down the highway my attention is arrested by electronic billboards.

Nicholas Carr nearly won the Pulitzer Prize for his book *The Shallows: What the Internet Is Doing to Our Brains*. In it, he recounts numerous conversations with very bright men and women, PhDs in their fields, who all confessed a similar phenomenon: the noticeable deterioration of their attention. Even though these intellectuals live and move in the world of books, research, literature, Carr was startled to corroborate so many reports that they couldn't read books anymore. Couldn't read articles, hadn't the patience even for a long blog post.[4] He goes on to document how the internet is reshaping not only our ability to take in information, it is altering the structures of our brains. We don't like being asked to focus on anything for very long anymore; we are adapted to the quick, short stimulus of the internet and our mobile devices.[5]

I think you know the zip, zip, zip effect all this is having on your attention. Part of what makes this troubling, Carr notes, is this:

> It's not only deep thinking that requires a calm, attentive mind. It's also empathy and compassion. Psychologists have long studied how people experience fear and react to threats, but it's only recently that they've begun researching the sources of our

nobler instincts. What they're finding is that, as Antonio Damasio, the director of USC's Brain and Creativity Institute, explains, the higher emotions emerge from neural processes that "are inherently slow. . . ."

The writer of a cover story in *New York* magazine says that as we become used to the "twenty-first-century task" of "flitting" among bits of online information, "the wiring of the brain will inevitably change . . ." We may lose our capacity "to concentrate on a complex task from beginning to end," but in recompense we'll gain new skills, such as the ability to "conduct 34 conversations simultaneously across six different media."

Carr's conclusion is worth repeating here:

The "frenziedness of technology," Heidegger wrote, threatens to "entrench itself everywhere." It may be that we are now entering the final stage of that entrenchment. We are welcoming the frenziedness into our souls.[6]

You already knew this from your own experience; your frenzied soul has been trying to tell you for some time. But we frogs don't yet see the real implications of this warming kettle.

1. Nicholas Carr notes how the "internet is reshaping not only our ability to take in information, it is altering the structures of our brains." How concerning is this to you?

2. Have you experienced a noticeable deterioration in your ability to focus and pay attention for long periods of time? When is this behavior most apparent?

3. How does the "frenziedness" of your soul impact your time with God and those you love?

DAY TWO: THE INABILITY TO LINGER

Down through the ages, followers of Christ have believed that to be able to give God our attention as a regular practice was a *very* important thing. After vividly recounting the many challenges of faith and character before us, the author of Hebrews says,

> Let us run with endurance the race God has set before us. We do this by keeping [fixing] our eyes on Jesus, the champion who initiates and perfects our faith (Hebrews 12:1–2, NLT).

I don't think we realize how much our use of technology and its assault on our attention has made this difficult to do. You can't give God your attention when your attention is constantly being targeted and taken captive . . . and you're cooperating.

In a blog post entitled "Mobile Blindness," marketing guru Seth Godin writes,

> We swipe instead of click, we scan instead of read, even our personal email. We get exposure to far more at the surface, but we rarely dig in. As a result, the fine print gets ignored. We go for headlines, not nuance. It's a deluge of gossip and thin promises . . . blog posts and tweets are getting shorter. We rarely stick around for the long version. "Photo-keratitis," "snow blindness," happens when there's too much ultraviolet, when the fuel for our eyes comes in too strong and we can't absorb it. Something similar is happening to each of us, to our entire culture as a result of the tsunami of noise vying for our attention.[7]

Mobile blindness. The quick pass. The inability to linger and dig deep. It's just the next thing, the next thing, the next thing. Our precious attention has been groomed and taken hostage. Let's contrast that with Psalm 1:1–4:

> *Blessed is the one*
>   *who does not walk in step with the wicked,*
> *or stand in the way that sinners take*
>   *or sit in the company of mockers,*
> *but whose delight is in the law of the LORD,*
>   *and who meditates on his law day and night.*
> *That person is like a tree planted by streams of water,*
>   *which yields its fruit in season,*

and whose leaf does not wither—
   whatever they do prospers.
Not so the wicked!
   They are like chaff
that the wind blows away.

Two types of people are being contrasted here, two types of experience: The first type is rooted and substantive and so life giving. Then there is the person so lacking in substance, so ephemeral that their reality is compared to dandelion puffs, chaff, that a breath of wind can sweep away. The key is this: the rooted person is able to meditate—*give sustained attention to*—the revelation of God. Not swipe, not multitask. Lingering focus. So Crawford wonders, "As our mental lives become more fragmented, what is at stake often seems to be nothing less than the question of whether one can maintain a coherent self. I mean a self that is able to act according to settled purposes and ongoing projects, rather than flitting about."[8]

Dear reader—you can't find more of God when all you're able to give him is a flit and flicker of your attention.

1. What does Hebrews 12:1–2 say is the key to running the race with endurance that God has set before us? How hard is that to do in this world of endless distractions?

2. In what ways do you encounter mobile blindness "as a result of the tsunami of noise vying for our attention"? What might you do to counter that?

3. How would you describe the two types of people mentioned in Psalm 1—and which do you most resemble in this season of life?

DAY THREE: IN LOVE WITH DISTRACTION

Stasi and I celebrated our thirty-fifth wedding anniversary with a trip to Kauai. We find it the most gorgeous of the Hawaiian Islands, maybe one of the most beautiful places on earth. Volcanic cliffs covered with lush tropical forest spill right down to the water's edge. Hibiscus blossoms fall onto the peaceful rivers that wind their way through the jungle. This isn't your tourist Hawaii. Apart from Princeville, the North Shore is way laid back, and after you cross a couple one-lane bridges, you feel you really could be on the outskirts of Eden.

Sitting on a quiet beach there, with no one to our right or left for more than two hundred yards of pristine white sand, it was so luscious I expected Adam and Eve to go strolling by any moment. Now, you'd think this would be enough to delight, enchant, and soothe any soul, but as I took a stroll down the beach myself, I passed a guy sitting under a banyan tree—watching videos on his iPhone.

Wow.

You can't unplug from your technology even in paradise?

Now, to be fair, I bet this is what happened: He had his phone with him—because everybody always has their phone with them—and somebody texted him a funny YouTube video, and he couldn't resist the urge, and that was that. He was glued to a little artificial screen watching some cat sit on a toilet, when all around him was beauty beyond description, the very beauty his soul needed, and filling that beauty and coming through it the presence of God.

And I saw myself in this guy.

Because I, too, had brought my phone with me to the beach, and I, too, responded when the little "chirp" alerted me to an incoming text. (We always have our excuses; every addict does. I was "keeping myself available to my children.") Every notification got my attention, because it triggered the brain's learned response to check out what news had just come in.

> Dopamine causes you to want, desire, seek out, and search. . . . It is the opioid system (separate from dopamine) that makes us feel pleasure. . . . The wanting system propels you to action and the liking system makes you feel satisfied and therefore pause your seeking. If your seeking isn't turned off at least for a little while, then you start to run in an endless loop [Dopamine Loop]. The dopamine system is stronger than the opioid system. You tend to seek more than

you are satisfied. . . . Dopamine starts you seeking, then you get rewarded for the seeking which makes you seek more. It becomes harder and harder to stop looking at email, stop texting, or stop checking your cell phone to see if you have a message or a new text. . . . The dopamine system doesn't have satiety built in. It is possible for the dopamine system to keep saying "more more more," causing you to keep seeking even when you have found the information.[9]

Neo was never so totally and completely trapped in the Matrix.

1. Have you been on vacation or in a setting to escape the noise of the world when your phone began chirping? What does it say about us that we often will come up with any excuse to not fully unplug—even for brief times of soul care?

2. How difficult would it be for you to turn off the constant interruptions of social media notifications—from your aunt posting another picture of her dog on Facebook to weather updates about a snowstorm across the country to the embarrassing thing the president just said? What are you most concerned about missing?

3. Have you recently found it hard to stop texting or checking for new messages—even when there's nothing urgent happening? How would you describe the effect of this dopamine loop when you're caught in it?

DAY FOUR: DENIAL

Since denial is one of the stages of addiction, let me ask you, dear reader, a couple questions: When your little chime, glass, or swoosh sound alerts you to an incoming text, do you easily ignore it and go on with the conversation you are having, or reading what you are reading, or enjoying the back seat view as you drive through the desert? I'm serious—when that thing vibrates in your pocket, do you regularly ignore it? Or do you automatically reach to see? Can you shut your phone off when you get home in the evening and not turn it on again until morning? When you first wake, do you allow yourself a leisurely coffee and bagel before you look at your phone—or is your phone the very first thing you look at every morning?

Yeah, me too. Let's be honest: we *prefer* distraction. The more distracted we are, the less present we are to our souls' various hurts, needs, disappointments, boredom, and fears. It's a short-term relief with long-term consequences. What blows my mind is how totally normal this has become; it's the new socially acceptable addiction. I've got a friend who decided to break with his; he now turns his phone off over the weekend. I text him, and he doesn't reply until Sunday night or Monday morning. I'm embarrassed by my irritation: *C'mon, man—you know the protocol. Everybody agrees to be totally available, anywhere, anytime, 24/7. It's what we do.*

What does it say that you look like some sort of nut job when you turn your phone off?

The brother of Jesus was trying to offer some very simple guidelines to a true life with God when, among other things, he said, "Religion that God our Father accepts as pure and faultless is this: to look after orphans and widows in their distress and to keep oneself from being polluted by the world" (James 1:27). That unpolluted part—that's what worries me, when the average American checks their phone eighty times a day (!), and 70 percent said they sleep with their phone within reach.[10]

1. Is it possible that you prefer distraction because it keeps you from your soul's fears, hurts, and disappointments? If so, can you name a few of the issues that you have been avoiding?

2. What might be the long-term consequences of these short-term choices for relief rather than restoration?

3. In the area of unplugging, what one change can you make to keep yourself from "being polluted by the world" (James 1:27)?

DAY FIVE: WE HAVE A CHOICE

Finding more of God, growing strong in soul and spirit, requires creating space in your day for God—to intentionally put yourself in a place that allows you to draw upon and experience the healing power of the life of God filling you. Over the ages, serious followers of Jesus have used stillness and quiet, worship, fasting, prayer, beautiful places, and a number of other "exercises" to drink deeply of the presence of God. And untangle their souls from the world.

The ongoing deluge of intriguing facts and commentary, scandal and crisis, genuinely important guidance combined with the latest insider news from around the globe, and our friends' personal lives gives the soul a medicated feeling of awareness, connection, and meaning. Really, it's the new Tower of Babel—the immediate access to every form of "knowledge" and "groundbreaking" information right there on our phones, every waking moment. It confuses the soul into a state of artificial meaning and purpose, all the while preventing genuine soul care and life with God. Who has time to read a book? Plant a garden?

Let me say it again, because it's so counter to the social air we breathe: what has become the normal daily consumption of input is numbing the soul with artificial meaning and purpose while in fact the soul grows thinner and thinner through neglect, harmed by the very madness that passes for a progressive life. We are literally being forced into the "shallows" of our life.

I'm not scolding; I'm tossing a lifeline.

Sincere followers of Jesus in every age have faced very difficult decisions—usually at that point of tension where their life with and for God ran straight against the prevailing cultural norm. The new Tower of Babel is ours. We have always been "strangers and aliens" in the world, insofar as our values seemed so strange and bizarre to those around us. We are now faced with a series of decisions that are going to make us look like freaks—choices like fasting from social media, never bringing our smartphones to any meal, conversation, or Bible study, cutting off our media intake so we can practice stillness every day.

The good news is that we actually have a choice. Unlike persecution, the things currently assaulting us are things we can choose not to participate in.

1. How do you currently create space for God each day? What new practices would you like to try to experience even more of God?

2. What does today's reading describe as the new Tower of Babel—and how does it confuse the soul?

3. Do you agree that we have a choice to participate or not participate in the things that are assaulting our souls? If so, what will you now choose to no longer participate in? If you disagree, why do you feel you have no choice?

RECOMMENDED READING

Before your group meets for the next session, we encourage you to read chapter 3, "Drinking Beauty," and chapter 7, "Get Outside," of Get Your Life Back. Those chapters will be the focus of session 3.

SESSION 3

GET OUTSIDE

"The world is charged with the grandeur of God."

GERALD MANLEY HOPKINS

WELCOME

Human beings need oxygen in order to live. Lots of it. So our loving God provided us a world completely engulfed in oxygen; we swim in life-giving air like fish swim in water. Put your arm out—it's surrounded with oxygen. Look down at your feet—they're wading through it too. God also arranged for the daily replenishment of this planet-wide ocean of oxygen, through the forests and jungles and even the algae of the seas. We take it in all day long, and all day long he renews it. Lavish. And a good thing too!

He's done the same with water. We need it daily. No human being can go without it for more than four days. Our planet is called the "blue planet" because of the amount of water we have. The oceans, of course, and the rain cycle that draws water from them and spreads it over the earth. Streams, ponds, rivers, lakes—the generosity of God can be seen here too. Without water nothing lives. Think of what happens to your lovely flowers when they are deprived of water.

Now, with the same generosity and care, God also filled the world with a renewable supply of something our souls need daily: beauty. Yes, beauty. The fact that our world is so saturated with beauty, breathtaking in so many ways great and small—this ought to let you know God feels it's something you need for your survival. We are absolutely swimming in it.

But apart from the artist and poet, most people don't intentionally pursue beauty as nourishment. Notice that beauty doesn't make the typical lists of discipleship models, spiritual disciplines, or soul care. Even in his wonderful, seminal book on healing trauma—*The Body Keeps the Score*—Dr. Bessel van der Kolk barely refers to it. That baffles me. Beauty is one of the richest graces God has provided to heal our souls and absorb his goodness.

One of the best things that happened to me this summer was the air conditioning going out in my truck. That truck's got a hundred sixty thousand miles on it, so I wasn't too upset. The shutdown forced me to drive with the windows down, which opened the world to me in a way I didn't even know I needed. They called it "Texas air conditioning" back in the day; cars used to come equipped with little triangular windows on both the driver and passenger sides, which flipped inward; people used them to force air in. You don't see those anymore because we prefer driving sealed in our little shell. As Robert Pirsig wrote in his '70s classic, *Zen and the Art of Motorcycle Maintenance*:

In a car you're always in a compartment, and because you're used to it you don't realize that through that car window everything you see is just more TV. You're a passive observer and it is all moving by you boringly in a frame.[11]

Driving with the windows down required me to drive a little slower, a good thing in itself, which allowed me to take in all the wonderful aromas of summer—hayfields, pine forest, wet pavement after a shower, rivers (yes, rivers have a very distinct fragrance; some coastal rivers smell like a bad fish market, but the rivers flowing down from high mountains have a lovely aroma I would call "forest nectar" or "green freshness"). I got to enjoying it so much I didn't get the air fixed for months.

GETTING STARTED

To kick off this week's session, discuss the following:

1. Beauty is all around us—songbirds, the grain of wood, a field of grass, the stars, water in almost any form. What aspect of beauty have you noticed today?
2. Do you receive beauty as a gift to your soul—or find God in the beauty? How might doing so help your soul to breathe?
3. What are some ways that you can fill your home with beauty and nature?

CORE SCRIPTURE

Invite someone to read aloud the following passage from Psalm 23. Listen for fresh insight and share any new thoughts with the group through the questions that follow.

> The LORD is my shepherd, I lack nothing.
> He makes me lie down in green pastures,

He leads me beside quiet waters,
He refreshes my soul.

—PSALM 23:1–3

1. Where does God take David to guide him into a soul restoring experience?

2. What aspects of beauty and nature are described in this passage?

3. How does God use beauty and nature to refresh your soul?

VIDEO TEACHING

Watch the video segment for session 3. A summary is provided for your benefit as well as space to take additional notes.

Summary

- As humans, we need oxygen and water to live. God gives us a planet saturated in both. He also gave us a world saturated in another grace that is absolutely essential to the human soul—beauty.

- Beauty restores the soul. It is a gift from God that heals, is merciful, and is kind. It assures us of God's abundance and reassures us that goodness wins over evil.

- We spend 93 percent of our lives in an artificial world—filled with plastic furniture, fake plants, synthetic carpet, fluorescent lights, and "air fresheners." This is life for people in a science-fiction novel, not the life God created for human beings.

- Technology—where most people live their lives—is draining. Nature is healing. So reduce one and increase the other.

- The good news is you don't have to go to the Alps or take a trip to Tuscany to experience nature and beauty. Simply get outside for five minutes and savor the world God made.

- One way to pursue soul care is to fill our homes with beauty.

- The secret of the healing power of beauty is learning to receive it as a gift. Receive it into your soul and, with it, receive God and his love and presence in your life.

Notes

GROUP DISCUSSION

Take a few minutes to go through the following questions
with your group.

1. Which of this session's two locations resonated more
   with you—the clean, modern studio set or the natural
   outdoor setting? Why?

2. Do you agree with the statement in the video that our
   world is far more beautiful than functional? Why or
   why not?

3. Have you considered how beauty—like oxygen or water—
   is an essential human need? What do you think happens
   to the soul when it is deprived of beauty for a prolonged
   period of time?

4. In what ways does beauty reveal the goodness of God's heart and his lavish abundance?

5. It's estimated we spend 93 percent of our lives indoors in an artificial environment. How does that statistic make you feel? What are some ways you can get outside and experience the richness of God's creation each day?

6. Casually glancing at something beautiful while you multitask isn't the same as pausing to receive beauty as a gift from God. How will the practice of receiving beauty into your soul help you get more of your life back?

CLOSING PRAYER

Wrap up your time together with prayer. Remember, prayer is simply talking to God. Here are a few ideas of what you could pray about based on the topics of this third session:

- Ask God to reveal a location outdoors for the two of you to spend time together.
- Pursue God through experiencing the beauty of his creation.
- Commit to spending time outdoors each day, away from the artificial.
- Pray for God to help you receive the healing power of beauty as a gift.
- Meditate on Psalm 23:1–3, personalizing the words as you speak them aloud.

GIVING IT A TRY

Nature heals, teaches, strengthens, soothes; it brings us the presence of God, for "The whole earth is filled with his glory" (Isaiah 6:3, NLT). This week's practice is to let nature restore your soul through three simple experiences. You can do this wherever you happen to find yourself. It doesn't need to be amazing and you don't have to go somewhere exotic. You just need to spend time outdoors.

- Touch nature. Seriously—every day, your soul needs to engage with creation. There's all sorts of research showing how healing this is.[12]

- Get outside, every day. If you work out in a gym, take it outside this week with a run, bike, swim, or hike. Turn off the AC and roll down the windows in your car. Walk around outside your home or office building every day.

- Encounter weather whenever you can. Don't hide from it; experience it. Walk in the rain. Step into the snow. Feeling the sun on your face, a breath of wind, the fresh kiss of snowflakes is resuscitating.

SESSION 3

─────

BETWEEN-SESSIONS
PERSONAL STUDY

In this section, you can further explore the material we've covered this week. If you haven't already done so, we encourage you to read chapter 3, "Drinking Beauty," and chapter 7, "Get Outside," of *Get Your Life Back* at this time. Each day offers a short reading from the book—along with reflection questions designed to take you deeper into the themes of this week's study. Journal or just jot a few thoughts after each question. At the start of the next session, there will be a few minutes to share any insights . . . but the primary goal of these questions is for your personal growth and private reflection.

DAY ONE: BEAUTY'S POWER

Beauty comforts. Beauty heals. Why else would we send flowers to a hospital room or funeral?

I've been personally convinced of this for years, so it was with delight I opened a lovely little book a friend recommended: *On Beauty and Being Just* by Harvard aesthetics professor Elaine Scarry. The author is trying to restore the high place of beauty in a skeptical world:

> Beauty is life-saving. . . . Augustine described it as "a plank amid the waves of the sea." Proust makes a version of this claim over and over again. Beauty quickens. It adrenalizes. It makes the heart beat faster. It makes life more vivid, animated, living, worth living. . . . It is as though one has suddenly been washed up onto a merciful beach.[13]

That's it—beauty rescues. It rescues because it is merciful, comforting. It heals, restores, revives, renews. This is why people in convalescence want to sit in a garden, or by a window overlooking the sea. Research shows that patients recovered faster, needed fewer pain killers, and left the hospital sooner if their windows allowed views of nature.[14] "The pleasure we take in beauty is inexhaustible," writes Scarry. "No matter how long beautiful things endure, they cannot out-endure our longing for them."[15]

Stasi and I were on a mission of sorts to the UK last spring, a whirlwind trip with something like nineteen engagements in nine days. We spent two nights in the London suburb of St. Albans, one of those trendy little British towns where cobblestones streets and fifteenth-century buildings meet art galleries and upscale restaurants. It was crowded, unusually hot, with lots and *lots* of traffic. My sensitivity was probably heightened by my exhaustion—and the exhaust— but the sound of motorcycles roaring up and down the narrow streets was really getting on my nerves. What was charming soon felt harming. At that moment I received a text from my wife, who had left the thoroughfare earlier to go in search of the cathedral: "Come to the cathedral; step inside."

As soon as I entered the garden-like grounds I began to feel better. Grass. Flowers. Trees. I stepped into the sanctuary and found myself alone. Coolness. Soft, colored light filtered down through the stained glass windows. The heavy stone structure held out every bit of city noise. Far up in front, hidden from view, the chapel choir was practicing. It was heavenly, and thus it was healing. Heaven always heals. Beauty heals, partly because it *proclaims* that there is goodness in the world and that goodness prevails, or is preserved, or will somehow outlast all harm and darkness.

1. When is the last time that beauty made your heart beat faster?

2. Can you think of a time that you saw—or experienced firsthand—the healing power of beauty? What was the object of beauty and how did it help bring restoration?

3. Professor Elaine Scarry says, "No matter how long beautiful things endure, they cannot out-endure our longing for them." What beauty do you find yourself longing most for—and why?

DAY TWO: A GENTLE GRACE

Beauty also sings to us songs of abundance.

I recently spent an afternoon seated in a camp chair high above a lake in the Wind River Mountains, simply drinking in the valley before me. The lake and granite cliffs were like Yosemite, gorgeous and grand, but my eyes were continually drawn to the evergreen forests on the mountain slopes. These are well-watered forests, so thick and lush it seemed I could see a million trees along a few miles of slope. My soul loved it, and I tried to pay attention to why. It had to do with abundance. One tree is a miracle; a hundred trees a celebration. But the staggering presence of tens of thousands of tall, thriving evergreens in dense profusion fills the soul with memories of Eden, visions that speak messages. "Beautiful things, as Matisse shows, always carry greetings from other worlds within them."[16] The Christian understands those greetings to come from the kingdom of God itself.

But most of all, beauty *reassures*. This is especially important to our search here for the grace beauty offers our life with God. We need reassuring.

Beauty reassures us that goodness is still real in the world, more real than harm or scarcity or evil. Beauty reassures us of abundance, especially that God is absolutely abundant in goodness and in life. Beauty reassures us there is plenty of life to be had. I believe beauty reassures us that the end of this Story is wonderful. The French impressionist Matisse "repeatedly said that he wanted to make paintings so serenely beautiful that when one came upon them, suddenly all problems would subside."[17]

Beauty is such a gentle grace. Like God, it rarely shouts, rarely intrudes. Rather it woos, soothes, invites; it romances and caresses. We often sigh in the presence of beauty as it begins to minister to us—a good, deep soul-sigh.

1. Do you pay attention to what your soul loves? If so, can you name something that soothed it recently?

2. In what ways does beauty reassure us that goodness is still real in the world?

3. Have you considered beauty as a "gentle grace" before now? How might seeing it in this way increase your appreciation for it?

DAY THREE: PLASTIC WRAP

I ran across a news release so shocking I had to read it twice. It didn't make the front page, but it should have: the average person now spends 93 percent of their life indoors (this includes your transportation time in car, bus, or metro).[18] Ninety-three percent—such a staggering piece of information. We should pause for a moment and let the tragedy sink in.

That means if you live to be 100, you will have spent 93 of those years in a little compartment and only 7 outside in the dazzling, living world. If we live to the more usual 75, we will spend 69 and three-fourths of our years indoors, and only 5 and one-fourth outside. This includes our childhood; how does a child be a child when they venture outside only a few months of their entire childhood?

This is a catastrophe, the final nail in the coffin for the human soul. You live nearly all your life in a fake world: artificial lighting instead of the warmth of sunlight or the cool of moonlight or the darkness of night itself. Artificial climate rather than the wild beauty of real weather; your world is always 68 degrees. All the surfaces you touch are things like plastic, nylon, and faux leather instead of meadow, wood, and stream. Fake fireplaces; wax fruit. The atmosphere you inhabit is now asphyxiating with artificial smells—mostly chemicals and "air fresheners"—instead of cut grass, wood smoke, and salt air (is anyone weeping yet?). In place of the cry of the hawk, the thunder of a waterfall, and the comfort of crickets, your world spews out artificial sounds—all the clicks and beeps and whir of technology, the hum of the HVAC. Dear God, even the plants in your little bubble are fake. They give no oxygen; only the plastic off-gases toxins, and if that isn't a signal fire I don't know what is.

This is a life for people in a science fiction novel. This would be understandable, acceptable, if we'd colonized Mars and by necessity you lived in a bubble. But this is not the life God ordained for the sons of Adam and the daughters of Eve, whose habitat is this sumptuous earth. It's like putting wild horses in a Styrofoam box for the rest of their lives.

You live a bodily existence. The physical life, with all the glories of senses, appetites, and passions—this is the life God meant for us. It's through our senses we learn most every important lesson. Even in spiritual acts of worship and prayer we are standing or kneeling, engaging bodily. God put your soul in this amazing body and then put you in a world perfectly designed for that experience. Which is why the rescue of the soul takes place through our engagement with the real world.

Living in an artificial world is like spending your life wrapped in plastic wrap. You wonder why you feel tired, numb, a little depressed, when the simple answer is you have a vitamin D deficiency; there's no sunlight in your life, literally and figuratively.

Our body, soul, and spirit atrophy because we were made to inhabit a real world, drawing life, joy, and strength from it.

To be shaped by it, to relish in it. Living your days in an artificial world is like living your whole life with gloves on, a filtered experience, never really feeling anything. Then you wonder why your soul feels numb.

1. What is described above as "a catastrophe, the final nail in the coffin for the human soul"?

2. Look around you as you read this. How much of your world would you say is artificial? List as many items as you can in the space below.

3. This reading includes the statement that "the rescue of the soul takes place through our engagement with the real world." Can you give an example of how this has been true for you? If it hasn't yet, would you like it to be?

4. Did you realize how soul-numbing time spent in an artificial world could be? What can you begin doing to get more sunlight in your life?

DAY FOUR: GOD IS OUT THERE

We are looking for more of God. You're far more likely to find him in a walk through an orchard or a sit by a pond than you are in a subway terminal. Of course God is with us and for us wherever we are, but in terms of refreshment, renewal, *restoration*, in terms of finding God in ways we can drink deeply of his wonderful being, you'd do better to look for him in the cry of the gull than the scream of the siren. God inhabits the world he made; his vibrancy permeates all creation:

The whole earth is filled with his glory! (Isaiah 6:3, NLT).

Christ . . . ascended higher than all the heavens, so that he might fill the entire universe with himself (Ephesians 4:9–10, NLT).

In the most beloved of Psalms, perhaps the most beloved of all Scripture, David wrote a poem to celebrate the restoration of his soul. Notice that God took him into nature to accomplish that:

The LORD is my shepherd, I lack nothing.
   He makes me lie down in green pastures,
he leads me beside quiet waters,
   he refreshes my soul (Psalm 23:1–3).

Be careful you don't dismiss this as something belonging to an agrarian age. God could have taken David into the palace to renew him; he could have taken him into the home of a friend or family member; he could have chosen the bustling markets of Jerusalem. In other words, there were plenty of indoor options for God to employ. But his choice for David's resuscitation was nature, his greenhouse, filled with his own life, pulsing with his glory, unique in its ability to restore and renew his children.

The rescue is always close at hand. The Spirit of God still hovers over creation; nature is ever renewed with "the dearest freshness." There's nothing better for a fried soul than to get in the woods or walk in the park. Lie on your back in the grass and watch the clouds go by. Sit on the beach and watch the breakers.

Recently I was on a two-week business trip; it began with an overnight flight, ten hours in a tube. From there it was airports, hotels, cars—an entirely artificial existence. Everything was fake—weather, lighting, sounds. On the last night, a massive thunderstorm let loose in the city. My car was parked two blocks away. Instead of trying to avoid the rain by calling a cab, or cringing and moping at the fact that I would get utterly soaked, I *relished* it. I rejoiced the entire two torrential blocks; I whooped and shouted and let the rain utterly douse me. After days upon days in the artificial, it was a cleansing baptism.

1. While God is everywhere, do you tend to experience more of God's presence outdoors or indoors?

2. When is a recent example where this happened?

3. In Psalm 23:1–3, do you think the setting is relevant to the transformation David experienced? Why or why not?

DAY FIVE: ALLOWING NATURE TO HEAL

I recently had a fried-soul kind of day. One where everything seems to go sideways from the moment you get out of bed; I'll bet you've had one of these:

There's no milk, so there's no cereal, and you're late anyway, so there's no breakfast. You're halfway to work when you realize you forgot your phone—so you're late to work because you went back and got your phone and now you're behind on everything. People are tweaked at you. You look forward to lunch as your first chance to come up for air, but the line at your favorite taco joint is out the door, and though you should have stayed, you're already well on your way to totally fried, so you leave in frustration, which only makes you skip lunch, which justifies your use of chocolate and caffeine to see you through the afternoon. But that completely takes your legs out from under you, and all you end up accomplishing is making a list of the things you need to do, which overwhelms you. By the time you get home, you are seriously fried.

I was strung out, deep in a vat of anger, frustration, self-indulging cynicism, and fatigue. A dangerous place to be. The next move would be rescue or the knockout punch. After a cold dinner I went out on the porch and just sat there. I knew I needed rescue, and I knew the nearest hope of that was the porch.

It was a beautiful Indian summer evening, the kind where the heat of the day has warmed the breezes, but you can also feel the cool from the mountains beginning to trickle down like refreshing streams. Nature began its gentle work.

My heart started coming to the surface, as it often does when I can get away into nature and let beauty have its effect on me. Mind you—I didn't get to the beach. I'm not canoeing some mountain lake. I'm simply sitting on my back porch. It doesn't take much; rescue is always at hand. Warm summer evening, cool breeze, beautiful sky now turning that deep navy blue just before dark, crickets making their eternal melodies.

That's when the carnival started.

A beer would make this a lot better, went the voice. *Or maybe tequila. You oughta go find some cookies.* Some agitated place in me started clamoring for relief. It felt like two kingdoms were vying for my soul. The carnival was offering relief. Nature was offering restoration. They are leagues apart, my friends. Leagues apart.

Relief is momentary; it's checking out, numbing, sedating yourself. Television is relief. Eating a bag of cookies is relief. Tequila is relief. And let's be honest—relief is what we reach for because it's immediate and usually within our grasp. Most of us turn there, when what we really need is *restoration.*

Nature heals; nature restores. Think of sitting on the beach watching the waves roll in at sunset and compare it to turning on the tube and vegging in front of *Narcos* or *Fear the Walking Dead.* The experiences could not be farther apart. Remember how you feel sitting by a small brook, listening to its little musical songs, and contrast that to an hour of HALO. Video games offer relief; nature offers restoration.

This is what David was trying to put words to when he reported finding God in green meadows and beside quiet waters, emerging with a refreshed soul. Or as another translation has it, "He renews my strength" (Psalm 23:3, NLT). The world we live in fries the soul on a daily basis, fries it with a vengeance (it feels vengeful). We need the immersion David spoke of.

So I stayed on the porch, choosing to ignore the chorus of vendors trying to get me to leave in search of some relief. I knew if I left, all I would find was sugar or alcohol, and my soul would be no better for it. So I chose to let the evening continue to have its healing ministry.

Remember—God doesn't like to shout. His invitations are much more gentle.

Sunset was over; night was falling, and still I sat there. The evening itself was cool now, and an owl was hooting somewhere off in the distance. I could feel my soul settling down even more; the feeling was like unwrinkling or disentangling on a soul level, as your body does in a hot tub. *Thank you for this gift of beauty*, I said. *I receive it into my soul.*

Darkness, crickets, coolness, quiet. I felt like I'd been through detox. When I fell into bed that night, it was as if the hellish day had never even happened. Restoration. So much better than mere relief.

1. Can you recall a recent day in your life where everything went sideways from the moment you got out of bed? What were some of the factors that caused things to spiral downward?

2. In the midst of that difficult time, what would momentary relief have looked like? Now, what would real restoration look like?

3. Which option did you choose . . . and what was the result?

RECOMMENDED READING

Before your group meets for the next session, we encourage you to read chapter 10, "Caring for Neglected Places in Your Soul," of *Get Your Life Back*. That chapter will be the focus of session 4.

SESSION 4

CARING FOR NEGLECTED PLACES IN YOUR SOUL

"If you have raced with men on foot and they have worn you out, how can you compete with horses? If you stumble in safe country, how will you manage in the thickets by the Jordan?"

GOD, JEREMIAH 12:5

WELCOME

Last spring my dear wife left town for seven days. She was in great need of some personal time away, soul care, time alone with God. Which left me at home with the dogs, horses, normal household chores, and my work. *And* . . . an empty house, with evenings to do whatever I wanted. I pictured myself in all sorts of masculine bachelor rhapsody: hours of cable television, watching premier soccer and hunting shows; cereal for dinner; dressing from laundry still in heaps on the couch.

After I got home from dropping Stasi off at the airport, I kicked off my shoes and looked around, wondering which of the personal joys to begin with. That's when God stepped in. *Get out your journal*, he said. Now, to be fair, getting some time with God was on my agenda too. Absolutely. I just didn't have it taking place quite so suddenly. Maybe after that pastrami sandwich and the second half of the Liverpool game. I stood in the middle of the living room, a man vacillating between clarity and denial. Maybe I hadn't heard a thing.

Get out your journal, Jesus repeated. *You have neglected your soul.*

A long sigh. That I knew—my soul *felt* neglected. I slowly walked to my office to retrieve my journal and returned to the living room where I sat down: the guilty schoolboy who knows he's been slouching on his assignments, is not too happy to be found out, and is repentant enough to sit ready with pen in hand, wondering where the Master was going next.

"Where have I neglected my soul, Lord?" I asked.

In your ungrieved griefs, he replied.

Another sigh. My, he was moving quickly. Oh, I knew he was right. I mean, this wasn't anywhere on my radar, but once Jesus named it, I knew it was the missing thing—the overlooked and unattended place. (Sometimes it takes someone else to name the thing right in front of us that we cannot see.) Soccer and hunting shows were not going to address my real needs.

So I began to write out a list of losses and disappointments from the past eighteen months. It wasn't at all heavy or dark; it was cathartic. The relief in simply naming things was palpable. For the grief, or disappointment, or sadness is in there, recognized or not, and it takes a lot of energy to keep it below the surface. Letting it rise, naming its sources, is relieving. That beach ball we've been trying to hold underwater gets to pop up, and we don't have to suppress it anymore.

Your soul is a beautiful instrument, like a cello or piano, capable of a vast range of expression and experience. Over time, strings get broken, keys are lost. Thirty years of this, and there isn't much of us left with which to make music. Though we want God, he is forced to play one or two notes; it's all he has to work with. By attending to the neglected places of our souls, we recover the lost strings and damaged keys. The more we do, the more rich and colorful our lives become, because God has so much more to make music with.

GETTING STARTED

To begin this session, read the following excerpt from chapter 10 of *Get Your Life Back* and then discuss the questions that follow: "We run from pain, run back to our normal lives, try to pretend we aren't bereaved, bereft, whatever the loss may be. The problem is, we are running from huge tracts of our own soul, leaving them behind, and we can't find more of God because we are looking with so little of our own soul. It takes more of you to find more of God."

1. Have you been running—or putting off—certain unattended areas of your life?
2. Can you name one neglected area of your soul?
3. Have you realized how this may be getting in the way of finding more of God?

CORE SCRIPTURE

Invite someone to read aloud the following passage from Psalm 34. Listen for fresh insight and share any new thoughts with the group through the questions that follow.

The Lord is close to the brokenhearted
and saves those who are crushed in spirit.

—Psalm 34:18

1. What two conditions does this verse recognize about people?

2. What promises are made for those in this state?

3. Have you invited God into the neglected places of your soul yet? If not, can you name what is holding you back?

VIDEO TEACHING

Watch the video segment for session 4. A summary is provided for your benefit as well as space to take additional notes.

Summary

- God invites us to enter into the neglected places so that we can experience restoration in those areas of our lives.

- We often fail in our search to get our lives back and experience more of God because we are looking with so little of ourselves. The more setbacks and disappointments we experience, the more we leave parts of our soul behind.

- In John 21, Jesus has an encounter with Peter in which he goes after the unaddressed issues of Peter's soul. He had denied Jesus three times and was weighed down with grief, shame, and self-hatred. Through his three questions, Jesus pushes into those neglected areas so Peter can be restored. Jesus does the same for us.

- This mad world is never going to encourage you to take care of the neglected places in your soul. It never offers adequate time to grieve or heal from your losses.

- We can use the One Minute Pause to invite God into relational disappointment, lost dreams, or career frustrations. He will reveal the places we've neglected our soul.

- In Revelation 3:20, Jesus says he stands at the door and knocks. If anyone hears his voice and opens the door, he will come in. The door opens from the inside because we have a role to play in our healing. Jesus waits for us to give him permission to restore our losses, disappointments, and unattended griefs.

- A powerful soul care practice is to create two lists— things that bring healing to your soul and things that are harmful to it. Title one list "Helpful" and the other "Unhelpful" and list under each things that bring life or steal life from your soul.

Notes

GROUP DISCUSSION

Take a few minutes to go through the following questions with your group.

1. What stood out to you in the video session about new ways to see or care for the neglected places in your soul?

2. Describe a situation where you ignored a pressing need—a car repair, a difficult work conversation, a potential health issue—hoping the issue would somehow magically fix itself or go away. What was the result of this choice?

3. Have you also neglected places in your soul that need attention? If so, can you name a specific area where you'd like to pursue soul restoration (perhaps an area God revealed to you during this session's One Minute Pause)?

4. What stood out to you in the story of Jesus going after the broken places in Peter three times (John 21)? Why was this part significant to you?

5. Name five things that are lifegiving and helpful to your soul. Now, name five things that would fall in the unhelpful category because they are depleting.

6. Now, with which of these two categories do you spend the most time in an average week—and is a change needed?

CLOSING PRAYER

Wrap up your time together with prayer. Remember, prayer is simply talking to God. Here are a few ideas of what you could pray about based on the topics of this fourth session:

- Express your desire for more of God.
- Ask Jesus to reveal the neglected places in your soul that need attention.
- Name these losses and admit to yourself (and God) that they matter.

- Commit to step into those areas with him to pursue your healing.
- Invite God into your grieving process.
- Pray that God will help you treat your soul with kindness as you pursue restoration.

GIVING IT A TRY

This week's practice involves becoming more present to your own soul, to places that were left behind. To begin, pick one thing you would call a loss or disappointment that you feel you've had to put aside because there wasn't time or space to deal with it when it happened.

- Write the loss down. What was lost—a friendship, a hope, an opportunity that might have shaped your future? It's so important to name it.

- Has a movie or song brought you to tears recently? Play it again, and pay attention—why? What is this awakening in you? Put some words to it. The neglected losses are in there; give them a voice.

- Allow your soul to *feel*. Don't tell it what to feel; it knows what to do. Just give it permission. It might be anger at first, or it might be sadness, loneliness, *why bother*? You might find yourself shouting some profanities—*that's okay*. Your losses matter. Don't edit yourself into silence. Anger is a pretty common first reaction to unattended loss. Let it out. Grab a kitchen spatula and start whacking the pillows on your couch, all the while naming why you are so angry over this loss.

- Invite Jesus in. Invite his love, his comfort, his presence into this specific loss, for his presence brings mercy and healing. I find it important to ask, "What do you have to say about this, God? What are you saying to me about my losses?" His comforting words of interpretation, or promise, are part of the healing.

As you enter into this practice, it's important to remember you can't stand at a distance from your own soul and ask Christ to "go in there and deal with it." This isn't hostage negotiation; we don't hide a block away and hope God takes care of business. This is your own soul we're talking about; the door opens from the inside.

"I stand at the door and knock," Jesus explained. "If anyone hears my voice and opens the door, I will come in" (Revelation 3:20). We open the door to our soul *from the inside*. This is the purpose of naming the loss, feeling it, allowing ourselves to return to the place in our own being that we walked away from. We must enter these places ourselves—the memory, the emotion, whatever it is we are aware of. We *inhabit* our own soul again. Jesus insists on it. Once there, we open the door from the inside, inviting Christ in, which he is always so eager to do.

SESSION 4

~ ~

BETWEEN-SESSIONS PERSONAL STUDY

In this section, you can further explore the material we've covered this week. If you haven't already done so, we encourage you to read chapter 10, "Caring for Neglected Places in Your Soul," of *Get Your Life Back* at this time. Each day offers a short reading from the book—along with reflection questions designed to take you deeper into the themes of this week's study. Journal or just jot a few thoughts after each question. At the start of the next session, there will be a few minutes to share any insights . . . but the primary goal of these questions is for your personal growth and private reflection.

DAY ONE: AVOIDANCE

Our son's childhood bedroom was in the basement, directly beneath the upstairs bathroom. When you flushed the toilet or drained the bath, it sounded like water was running down through the walls. Almost like a Disney attraction. One day

I noticed that the toilet upstairs had gone quite loose on its setting, and it made me nervous. *How long has it been like that?* I immediately went downstairs to the bedroom and looked up at the ceiling . . . sure enough, there was a small but noticeable water stain. *Gadzooks.*

I fetched a ladder from the garage, along with a small tool for cutting drywall, and proceeded to test the ceiling for how far the damage had gone. I was expecting the worst (we always fear the worst) and wouldn't have been surprised if, after a little poking around, a three foot square of ceiling dropped out, toilet and plumbing with it. Much to my relief, the water leak appeared to be intermittent (the drywall was not soaked, only stained), and I knew the next step was to replace the section of ceiling and reseat the toilet with a new gasket and bolts. But I postponed doing so.

For one year.

That's right—an entire year. It slipped my mind. To be fair, I really did forget; to be *honest,* I was in denial. I didn't want to take on that project, so it was easy to let it "slip from my mind."

It's human nature to want our problems to simply go away. Be honest now—how many of us have heard a troubling *tick, tick, tick* or *thump, thump, thump* coming from the general direction of our car's engine or transmission and not done a thing about it, hoping it would just go away? We do this with our health all the time—that painful little hitch, the lump, the troubling indigestion, those few extra pounds cry for our attention, but we let it pass for months or even years, hoping it will magically sort itself out.

How much more our souls. In this busy, mad, distracted world, it's just too easy (and far more efficient) to send your soul to the back of the bus. Low priority. Maybe later. But you, my reader, have read this far, and I'm so proud of you! You're making the hard choices that will bear fruit for years and years to come.

1. It's human nature to want our problems to go away, but they rarely do so on their own. Why do you think God has made the world in a way where things don't just magically sort themselves out?

2. How has your soul been given low priority in this mad, distracted world?

3. How passionate are you to start focusing more attention to the neglected places in your soul?

DAY TWO: FINDING MORE OF GOD

It takes more of *you* to find more of God.

That's a big idea, so let me explain. My first dog was a Great Pyrenees–Border Collie mix, a big smart dog that looked like a wolf and played like a puppy. His name was Joshua. Never once in his life was he on a leash. He was the best dog I ever had, and when I lost him, I didn't know if I ever wanted another.

Years later we got Scout, our first family dog, a big male Golden Retriever who loved hiking, canoeing, and underwear. He was a great dog; losing him was heartbreaking, and I found myself giving less of my heart to our next Golden, Oban, who we lost this fall. Now we have a female Golden named Maisie, and I'm aware she has even less of me. Over time, each loss causes us to offer less and less next time. What's available in us is lessened through our losses.

We often can't find the more of God we long for, because we are looking with so little of ourselves. Too much of us has been left behind. Just as the assault on our attention keeps pushing us into the shallows, so we no longer hear deep calling unto deep, the pace of life rushes us past significant moments of disappointment and loss, and in doing so continues the "shallowfication" of our souls. We are like eroded stream banks, a little more shaved off every year. Or like the lonesome hero in "Desperado," who was losing all his "highs and lows" as his feelings simply went away.

So this is a good place to push back. We may have neglected our soul's need for beauty. We may have neglected our soul's need for play. But I have reason to believe that unattended loss is a good place to start if you would recover and heal the vessel God *wants* to fill, if you would open up room in your life for him to meet you there.

1. "We often can't find the more of God we long for, because we are looking with so little of ourselves. Too much of us has been left behind." In your own words, what do you think this statement means?

2. Can you relate to how more loss causes us to offer less and less in future situations? What is an example where you've experienced this firsthand?

3. How do you think loss and disappointment lead to the further "shallowfications" of our souls? How, specifically, has that been the case in your life?

DAY THREE: YOUR LOSSES MATTER

We live in a brutal world. Do I really need to convince anyone of this?

A world like this damages your soul as a matter of daily business. We must live wisely in return.

A colleague was reeling under the news of the loss of a childhood playmate. "Give yourself three months," I said. This is my standard line for grief. Not because it's a magic number, but because it's long enough to be realistic and short enough that people just might listen. No one enjoys hanging around grief. We want it to go away as quickly as possible, like an alcoholic uncle who chain-smokes in your house and makes loud, inappropriate comments, and all you want is for him to leave.

The madness about grief is you think you'll feel better in a few days. Certainly in a few weeks. The average bereavement leave in corporate America is four days for a spouse or child and three days for a parent.[19] Three days. That's complete insanity. It communicates an illusion that's totally detached from reality. At three days you haven't even begun to breathe. At four days you are still in total concussive shock. So I suggest three months of margin and soul care to someone in grief, because it shatters that illusion and suggests an open space of time where real grieving and healing can begin. *Begin*. Because who knows how long it really will take.

This cannibalistic world isn't going to say this to you, sure isn't going to act like it, so allow me to say it: your losses matter.

Oh, what kindness we begin to practice when we act like our losses matter.

This is why part of my soul-care regimen now includes a baseball bat and plastic trash bin. Our neighborhood requires the bins provided by the trash company; they are large, awkward, and nearly indestructible. Which make them perfect for hammering on with a baseball bat. Loss, disappointment, grief, and injustice provoke anger, and you've got to have somewhere to take it. (As a therapist, I've found suppressed anger morphs into fear, which is no better.)

I like to go out and give my bin a good thrashing when I'm in touch with the hurt and anger, the thievery and loss. (I do recommend closing the garage door if you can; you might alarm the neighbors.) We must do something with our rage. And let me add—of course you're angry. Your rage is not a sign that something's wrong with you; there's something wrong with the world. In some ways, everything is wrong with the world. We're often embarrassed by our anger, but it's simply proof that our hearts are aching for things to be *right*.

1. Society doesn't know how to handle grief, wanting it to be over as soon as possible. What does it say about our lack of soul care that the average bereavement leave in corporate America is just four days for a spouse or child and three days for a parent?

2. We begin to practice kindness when we act like our losses matter. How can you begin to show your soul more kindness in dealing with current and past loss?

3. Have you considered that your anger at loss is simply proof that your heart is aching for things to be *right*? How would understanding this fact change the way you process disappointment, grief, and the injustice you see?

DAY FOUR: THE EXTENT OF YOUR LOSSES

Stasi left for seven days, and Jesus seized the moment to take me into my losses, because I'd treated them like the leaky bathroom—with total neglect. He invited me first to name them and then, one by one, invite his healing love into these places. Some were great—the loss of a dear friend to cancer—and some were small. My intended week of kicking back and taking it easy turned into something so much more kind and healing.

As Mark Twain said, it takes years before you know the extent of your loss:

A man's house burns down. The smoking wreckage represents only a ruined home that was dear through years of use and pleasant associations. By and by, as the days and weeks go on, first he misses this, then that, then the other thing. And, when he casts about for it, he finds that it was in that house. Always it is an essential—there was but one of its kind. It cannot be replaced. It was in that house. It is irrevocably lost. He did not realize that it was an essential when he had it; he only discovers it now when he finds himself balked, hampered, by its absence. It will be years before the tale of lost essentials is complete, and not till then can he truly know the magnitude of his disaster.[20]

There is the initial loss, but as time goes by there are all the other losses: no one to call when you want to talk about that thing the two of you used to talk about, no one to share the joy when your favorite team wins. There's just an emptiness in your life now. I had grieved the initial loss, but what I was totally ignoring were all the other things lost in the burning down of that house.

1. If Jesus invited you to name your losses one by one, would you be able to do so? If so, list them below and then, one by one, invite his healing love into those places.

2. Mark Twain says that it takes years before we know the extent of our losses. Do you agree with his words? Why or why not?

3. We are often unprepared for the general emptiness that follows an initial loss. Can you recall a situation where the full magnitude of a loss wasn't realized until later? What are ways you can care for your soul throughout the grieving process?

DAY FIVE: HELPFUL AND UNHELPFUL

I began to take note of what helped me during that week and what hurt. Now, I realize that in my tenderness I was in a heightened state of sensitivity, but I found it revealing for that very reason—I could tell immediately what helped my dear soul, what did not, and what was bordering harmful. It was an epiphany; half the stuff we do to ourselves on a daily basis is actually pretty hurtful.

Television hurt. Even though I usually enjoy vegging out over my shows, I couldn't do TV. It was abrasive, like someone shouting at you when you've just broken an eardrum. Isn't that fascinating? It simply didn't feel nourishing. I mentioned earlier the research indicating that simply watching traumatic events can be traumatizing to the soul—and if you consume any TV at all, you've seen thousands of traumatic events.

I tried watching *Gladiator*. Normally, I love that movie. When I turned the channel on, the scene unfolding happened to be one of the big coliseum battle scenes. Part of me was drawn into the moment; a deeper part of my soul cringed; I had to turn it off. Hmmm . . . it made me wonder what I normally subject my soul to.

I needed to give up stimulants. Nicotine, caffeine, sugar—all those things we use to prop up our daily happiness will, over time, burn out the soul. Because the soul can't always be "on." (I was in one of those gas station quick marts the other day, and I was shocked at the size of the cooler devoted to energy drinks. It used to just be Red Bull and a few others; now there are dozens and dozens, floor to ceiling. They take up more space than water. We are forcing our souls into a perpetual state of anxiety, and that is super damaging, like redlining your car's RPMs all the time.) The pace of life, lack of any transitions, and state of always being plugged into our phones and technology reduces our living to one continuous experience of being "on." That'll wipe you out for sure. The world does enough to fry your soul; you certainly don't want to add to it through overstimulation.

By contrast, the "graces" in this study guide are designed to help your soul come down from hypervigilant mode, or constant distraction, or the dopamine "loop"—whatever you are caught in. This allows your body, brain, and soul to calm down, to find Christ again.

There's an enormous difference between relief and restoration, as I said; much of what provided me relief in the past was not helping heal these neglected places I was intentionally surfacing. Allow me a brief list . . .

- Helpful: Generous amounts of sunshine. Everything living and green. Long walks. Lonesome country roads. Swimming. Beauty. Music. Water. Friendly dogs, (I've never understood it when someone says to me, "Yeah—we're not really dog people." That's like saying, "Yeah—we're not really happiness people.") Compassion. Not expecting myself to produce the same level of work I normally accomplish in a day. Yard work. Building a fence.

- Unhelpful: Grocery stores. Malls. Television. Traffic. Draining people wanting to talk to me. (Friends and family are at this moment wondering if they fall into this category. It's reserved for people who live out of touch with their own soul—and thus mine. "The way you treat your own heart.") Airports. The news—especially politics. Social media. Your typical dose of movie violence.

Now, which cluster of the things I've just named above make up most of your weekly routine? Do you begin to see more clearly how essential it is that we intentionally care for our neglected heart and soul?

My friends, I really don't want to be the unwelcome prophet, but the fact is this: life is not going to get better on this planet. It's going to get worse before it gets better; all signs indicate it's getting worse at an alarming rate. "If you have raced with men on foot and they have worn you out, how can you compete with horses? If you stumble in safe country, how will you manage in the thickets by the Jordan?" (Jeremiah 12:5). In other words, if you think this is hard, wait'll you see what's coming next. We're going to want our souls strong and ready for the days ahead, filled with God, not fried and empty. So we must practice soul care.

1. Are you aware of what helps and hurts your soul? Our choices often fall into the category of either relief or restoration. Give an example of a real-life choice you've made in each category—and the result from doing so.

2. The soul can't always be "on." What practices help your soul come down from hypervigilant mode, constant distraction, and the dopamine "loop" it gets caught in?

3. Do you tend to put the above practices into play daily, weekly, or only when it becomes a crisis? How can you make soul care a more proactive rather than reactive aspect of your life?

RECOMMENDED READING

Before your group meets for the next session, we encourage you to read chapter 8, "Remembering Who You Love," and chapter 13, "The Hidden Life of God in You," of *Get Your Life Back*. Those chapters will be the focus of session 5.

SESSION 5

THE HIDDEN LIFE
OF GOD IN YOU

"I have given them the glory that you gave me,
that they may be one as we are one — I in them and you
in me—so that they may be brought to complete unity."

JESUS, JOHN 17:22–23

WELCOME

"**I** need to get among the trees," a woman told me yesterday. "I need to be among trees again."

We were sharing things that restore our souls, and for her it is trees—groves, woodlands, forests, orchards. I nodded. Walking through a forest is about my most favorite thing to do: when the day is hot but it's cool under the canopy, when the light is filtering down through the leaves in broken patterns, changing colors like the light in a cathedral coming through the stained glass high above. I love walking along slowly, silently, when the mossy soil is moist and you tread without a whisper. The wildlife doesn't seem to mind your presence; you might see a fox or pine marten, the flank of a deer slipping into the high ferns. It feels like the entire forest is one living, breathing entity.

And it is.

For centuries, fairy tales and legends told of forests with mythical powers. Many indigenous peoples held certain groves to be sacred. We moderns found them charming, perhaps, but unscientific. Along comes the thoroughly researched but equally magical book *The Hidden Life of Trees* by a German forester, Peter Wohlleben. He stumbles across an ancient stump one day, which he first took to be a ring of moss-covered stones.

Looking closer, he discovers that the stump is still producing chlorophyll—something utterly impossible unless the trees around it were keeping it alive by sending it their own life. It led the forester into a series of dazzling discoveries about the interconnected life of the forest.[21]

When one tree in a forest is diseased, the other trees will send critical nutrition to it through the interconnection of the root system and fungi "network" in the forest floor, supporting the ill tree until it is well again.[22] Trees will also communicate with one another in this way. If a foreign invader like a beetle bores into one tree, that tree will send signals through the hidden connection in the humus, warning the others that an enemy has come; the forest responds by producing immune defenses, which they send up through their trunks and into their leaves.[23] Walking through a forest, the trees appear to be individuals, and they are. But there's an unseen shared life hidden from view, a connection of life and being I find beautiful and extraordinary.

This is very close to the interconnectedness God created each of us as individuals to have with him. I don't think our usual expressions of faith make this clear; they may even prevent us from seeking it.

GETTING STARTED

Begin this session with the group discussing the following:

1. Be honest. Does the topic of union with God sound like something reserved for the super-elite—perhaps those in full-time ministry or the leaders of your church? Why do you think that is?

2. Using everyday language, how would you describe this "unseen shared life" with God that we're invited into as a new believer?

3. Do you think our typical expressions of faith can get in the way of our seeking this deeper union with God? Why or why not?

CORE SCRIPTURE

Invite someone to read aloud the following passage from John 17. Listen for fresh insight and share any new thoughts with the group through the questions that follow.

> *I pray also for those who will believe in me through their message, that all of them may be one, Father, just as you are in me and I am in you. May they also be in us so that the world may believe that you have sent me. I have given them the glory that you gave me, that they may be one as we are one—I in them and you in me—so that they may be brought to complete unity.*
> —JOHN 17:20–23 (EMPHASIS ADDED)

1. Are you surprised to learn that this passage isn't primarily about church unity or getting along with each other—but actually about our hidden life with God?

2. How does that help you reinterpret what Jesus is inviting us into?

3. What two words does Jesus use to describe the primary goal? Given that, does it increase your hunger for the hidden life of God in you?

VIDEO TEACHING

Watch the video segment for session 5. A summary is provided for your benefit as well as space to take additional notes.

Summary

- John 17:20–23 is often interpreted as being primarily about church unity and unity with each other. While those are important things, the verse is actually about unity with God. That is the ultimate goal of human existence—a united life with God.

- Sadly, most believers have been given the impression that the sum total of the Christian life is faith, obedience, and service. These are all necessary and good things . . . but not the main invitation.

- Jesus invites us into something far more thrilling and beautiful and intimate than a life of Christian service. The intimacy that we can experience with God is absolutely wonderful.

- We need to remember the God we love. He is a God of beauty, wildness, power, generosity, and intimacy.

- God knows you really well. He knows your heart and what makes you come alive. He will drop reminders into your day that reveal his love for you—and that remind you of the God you love.

- A practice of loving God involves pausing throughout your day and saying, "You are amazing, God. This is who you are and what you're like. I love you."

- As you put this practice into action, it will actually open your soul up to greater union with God—which is the main thing we are after.

Notes

GROUP DISCUSSION

Take a few minutes to go through the following questions with your group.

1. How has this video session redefined your understanding of what union with God is—and isn't?

2. Did you grow up in a church or family where the main tenants were faith, obedience, and service? If so, what effect did that have on your heart and soul?

3. The enemy tries to distort our image of God. How has it been helpful for you to remember the God you love? What comes to mind when you do so?

How does knowing that Jesus wants to be intimately involved in your life and spend time together create a new expectancy for what this hidden life of God in you can be?

4. What was your experience like with the "intertwined life" hands practice? Did it provide a new way to understand the meaning of the passage in John 17?

5. What are some new ways you want to tell God you love him based on who he is and what he does?

CLOSING PRAYER

Wrap up your time together with prayer. Remember, prayer is simply talking to God. Here are a few ideas of what you could pray about based on the topics of this fifth session:

- Express your deep desire for a hidden life with God.
- Present yourself to God for greater union with him.
- Release everything else that's taking up room in your soul.
- Tell God how he is amazing by naming who he is and what he does.
- Pray John 17:20–23 to God, agreeing with it and asking for more of this reality.
- Ask God to remind you of his love for you in fresh, unexpected ways.

GIVING IT A TRY

The basic things we practice, the things that are at the top of our to-do list, should be things that help us find union with God. In this week's exercise, our goal is greater unity with God.

Step one is understanding that God wants union with you, that union is the purpose of your creation, that it's the priority. This is a good starting point; it's a massive reorientation.

Step two is presenting ourselves to God for union. I do this every day: "I present myself to you, God, for union with you." We pray for union; we ask for it. I ask for it during the One Minute Pause.

Step three (and this isn't science, folks, it's poetry; these "steps" are simply for clarity's sake) is to move toward a greater release of everything else taking up room in your soul. This is how we love the Lord our God with *all* our heart, soul, mind, and strength. "I give everyone and everything to you *for union with you.*"

As we move in and out of the various pressures and crises of life, we ask God to heal our union with him. The above practice will prove immensely helpful on that front.

SESSION 5

BETWEEN-SESSIONS PERSONAL STUDY

In this section, you can further explore the material we've covered this week. If you haven't already done so, we encourage you to read chapter 8, "Remembering Who You Love," and chapter 13, "The Hidden Life of God in You," of *Get Your Life Back* at this time. Each day offers a short reading from the book—along with reflection questions designed to take you deeper into the themes of this week's study. Journal or just jot a few thoughts after each question. At the start of the next session, there will be a few minutes to share any insights . . . but the primary goal of these questions is for your personal growth and private reflection.

DAY ONE: REMEMBERING WHO YOU LOVE

I received a text the other day from a friend of mine. It began as a surprising intrusion of joy, which grew into a rescue of my soul.

First came simply a photo, taken from the window of a bush plane somewhere in the Alaskan wilderness. At first glance, I couldn't quite make out what I was looking at. All I could see was a massive mountain slope, angling down toward a river. The impression was something far north and exotic. There are no trees in the photo, only tundra in autumn colors. The picture was taken from probably seventeen thousand feet, and something is dappling the surface of the tundra on both sides of the river. As my eyes adjusted, I realized I was looking at a massive assembly of living creatures, something out of Eden. While my mind tried to take in and sort out what I was beholding, the second text followed: "ninety thousand caribou stacked up for a river crossing." It filled my heart with joy—not only because I love wildness and massive animal migrations, but because it reminded me of the God I love.

And oh, how good it is to be reminded of the God we love—what he's really like, how generous his heart is.

I had a similar experience a few evenings later when Stasi and I were watching a BBC nature series on the oceans of our planet. Richly filmed in high definition, intimate and epic, the vast, colorful beauty of the seas, coasts, and coral lagoons saturating this planet was enough to evoke worship during every episode. The seven seas are gorgeous; talk about abundance! This particular episode was shot in the open ocean (utterly breathtaking) and a massive pod of dolphins began to fill the screen. Fifty . . . one hundred . . . one thousand dolphins all racing along in the open sea, twisting, leaping, diving in a sort of organized, whimsical chaos, racing along in pure dolphin happiness. The narrator explained we were watching a "super pod" of Atlantic dolphins *five thousand strong.* I was speechless; such things exist?! That encounter, that revelation was so holy that it removed in the moment every doubt I had in the goodness of God. *Right. This is the God I love,* I thought to myself. And my heart came back to him in tender hopefulness and affection.

We are talking about finding more of God. I assure you nothing, absolutely nothing, will bring you more of him than loving him. Turning our hearts toward God in love opens our being to receive him like no other practice. And it is a practice, something we consciously and actively engage in through the moments of our day-to-day. This is the epicenter of the book, really. The core truth from which all others flow. But I saved this session till now for several reasons. . . .

Most of my readers will be people of faith backgrounds, and as such, you have heard so many messages about love, loving God, God is love, that your soul has formed a kind of callous to the beauty of what such words reveal. We are too familiar with the conversation—almost, dare we admit, a little bored with it. So I waited until now to try unlocking this treasure because your soul needed some time to recover and heal through the practices we've looked at. We also needed the transition the preceding sessions have provided to help us disentangle from the world (including the religious world, which runs at basically the same pace as the rest of the mad world).

But I mostly forestalled this moment, this most essential of all truths, because our souls have built up some resistance to it through the disappointments of our lives, and we need to proceed with gentleness if we might open this, the greatest gift of all.

1. Have all the messages you've heard through life about love, God is love, and the love of God caused your soul to be a bit calloused to—or perhaps bored by—the beauty of these truths? Can you put into words how this happened or why you felt this way?

2. What reminds you afresh of the God you love—what he's really like and how generous his heart is?

3. Turning our hearts toward God in love opens our being to receive him like no other practice. How can you engage in this practice consciously and actively through the moments of your day?

DAY TWO: THE GOODNESS OF GOD

We need the clouds of sin and sadness melted away; we need the dark of our doubts driven off like night flees before dawn. So that the giver of immortal gladness might *fill us*.

Two simple practices will help you get there.

Start with something you love. The laughter of your child. Sunlight on the ocean. Your beloved dog. A favorite song, music itself. Perhaps a photo, like my caribou. A favorite spot—your garden, the cliffs at the sea, the family cabin. Someone dear to you. We begin with the things we love; this is the way back, the path home. For we don't always draw the connection—God made these specifically for you, and he gave you the heart to love them. You'll be out for a bike ride in the very early morning, cool breeze in your face, all the sweet, fresh aromas it brings, the exhilaration of speed, and your heart spontaneously sings, *I love this!* The next step is to say, *So does God. He made this moment; he made these things. He is the creator of everything I love.* Your heart will naturally respond by opening toward him.

It's like throwing your faith a lifeline: Every wonderful thing in your life is a gift from God, an expression of his heart toward you. All your precious memories, each and every one— your eighth birthday, when you got that little red bike that awakened your love of riding, which carried right on into your adult life. That perfect powder day, when you and your fiancé skied run after run, then warmed up by the fire in the lodge. The vacation you still think about, how fun it was, how carefree you felt. Your wedding reception: the dancing, the inextinguishable joy of it all. Every moment you have ever been happy, thrilled, comforted, hopeful . . . that was God loving you. Such gifts come from no other source. "You open your hand and satisfy the desires of every living thing. . . . Every good and perfect gift is from above, coming down from the Father" (Psalm 145:16; James 1:17).

No other act will bring you a greater measure of God than loving him, actively engaging your heart and soul in loving him. Because as we do, the flower of our being opens up to the sunshine of his presence and all the goodness he longs to breathe into us. The best way to get there is to think upon the things we love and remind ourselves, "This is from God; this is his true heart."

Because life is a savage assault on our heart's confidence that God is good—and thus our union with him—the practice of reminding ourselves he is the creator of everything we love will be a rescue of our faith.

Now, I'm not trying to put a Band-Aid over deep sorrow, suffering, trauma, or loss. Not for a moment. I'm not pretending that what those things have done to your relationship with God can be healed in a moment. But you'll be astonished and delighted by how much *can* be recovered in this first practice.

1. Think of something you love and write it below. How does knowing that God made the things we love specifically for us—and gave us the heart to love them—cause your heart to open to him in new ways?

2. "Have you considered that not just one or two things—but every moment you have ever been happy, thrilled, comforted, hopeful . . . that was God loving you?" How

does that enhance your understanding of this verse: "Every good and perfect gift is from above, coming down from the Father" (James 1:17)?

3. Life is a savage assault on our hearts' confidence that God is good—and thus our union with him. How might the practice of remembering that he is the creator of everything you love prove to be a rescue of your faith?

DAY THREE: AN OFFERING OF YOUR SUFFERING

There is a second practice that you will find equally helpful. Love God in your suffering.

Stay with me now. Your heart is the greatest treasure you have. Without a heart it's impossible to love, or receive love. Without a heart you can't possibly dream, hope, laugh, find courage. Without a heart you will never be happy. Your enemy knows this, knows he can use your suffering to both shut your heart down and turn you against God, if only subtly, in doubtful hurt. Listen to me carefully: *You must not let him.* You must guard your heart with everything you've got, especially in times of disappointment and pain. Your secret weapon against the enemy's hatred is to love God right then and there, in the midst of the sorrow, whatever it may be.

I recognize that the act of loving God often surfaces other things in our hearts, things that are currently in the way of our loving him. We might feel halfhearted in the act, and then we realize we feel hurt or distant from God, or that he feels distant from us. This is good; this allows us to bring to the surface and put words to things that are blocking the relationship. Naming those things is important. I will at this point either begin to write about it in my journal or simply say to Jesus, "I feel hurt about . . ." Then I will pray, "Come into this hurt, this feeling of abandonment, this numbness," or whatever seems to be thwarting your intimacy. "I love you here, God. I choose right here, in this, to love you."

Try it; you'll see.

I realize that sometimes these roadblocks are quite significant and may require more serious attention. You might need to process it with a counselor, or ask your spiritual leaders for prayer. But you want to work out the problems *while staying in the relationship*, not backing away from it—just like a married couple or good friends have to do. Your intimacy with God, this heart-to-heart love we were made for, this is *the* thing Satan most hates, and it has to be fought for.

When I'm feeling more disappointment than I am overflowing with reasons to love God, I turn to the things I know he has done on my behalf. "Thank you for creation," I'll say, because I love the world he's made, and I can at least start there—the meadows, waterfalls, caribou, dolphins.

"Thank you for creation." I continue, "Thank you for redemption"—for I know he loves me because of Jesus Christ: "God showed his great love for us by sending Christ to die for us while we were still sinners" (Romans 5:8, NLT). "Thank you for my redemption." And I will add, "Thank you for the coming kingdom," because it reminds me that my dreams *will* come true, any day now; goodness *is* coming to me. So when I'm trying to bring my heart along into the genuine act of loving God, I will pray, "Thank you for creation; thank you for redemption; thank you for the coming kingdom." My soul comes along as I do this, and I remember that I do in fact love God, whatever my current heartache may be.

This rescue helps your heart not pull away from the One Person who can heal you; it fortresses your heart against the lies of the enemy that rush in during heartbreak (*God doesn't love you; he's not good; you are alone; life is unfair*—all that). Actively choosing to love God in our pain allows us to receive the very grace the pain cries out for.

Let me give you an example. Some dear friends lost a child. That story is not mine to tell here. What I can say is that in their grief, they began to love God. "We still love you, God. We declare that you are good." All heaven was breathless; all hell was screeching in horror. Because they took away the enemy's weapon and turned it against him. It wasn't easy; there were still floods of tears. But they were not bitter tears, not angry or cynical, because they kept their hearts open to the One who could carry them through. Too many people pull away, walk through their pain alone, making it all the worse and lengthy. I can report that my friends' healing from the loss was much quicker because they chose this path, for it kept their souls open to God's presence, and he was, therefore, able to offer himself in healing love. They made an offering of their suffering.

Make an offering of your suffering. Love God in it.

1. Your heart is the greatest treasure you have. Look up and write Proverbs 4:23 in the space below. What most stands out to you about this verse?

2. Without a heart it's impossible to love or receive love. Without a heart you can't dream, hope, laugh, find courage. Your enemy knows this. Have you taken the care of your heart as seriously as you should? Why or why not?

3. What are some roadblocks currently in the way of you loving God with all your heart? Can you start the process of making an offering of your suffering in order to keep your soul open to God's presence?

DAY FOUR: WORDS FALL SHORT

Some readers will recall that Jesus used the imagery of a vine and its branches to describe the nature of connection he offers us (John 15). The branch is united with the vine, and that allows the vine to provide life in all its forms to the branch—sustenance, strength, immunity, resilience. The result for the branch is blossoming fruitfulness, abundant life. I'm afraid our familiarity with the passage, or at least the phrase "I am the Vine," has dimmed the miraculous offer: if you want, your life can become one shared existence with the Son of God, through whom all things were created, who sustains this glorious world.

Being the brilliant teacher he is, Jesus then followed up this metaphor with a second, one that ups the ante and drives home his sincerity with what was meant to be a startling comparison:

> I pray also for those who will believe in me through their message, that all of them may be one, Father, *just as you are in me and I am in you.* May they also be in us so that the world may believe that you have sent me. I have given them the glory that you gave me, *that they may be one as we are one*—I in them and you in me (John 17:20–23, emphasis added).

To be clear, Jesus prayed that we would experience the same kind of united life and being with him that he experienced with his Father. He reinforced how serious he is about this by asking his disciples to record this prayer for you, so that the startling force of it would be with us always, in black and white.

Over time, this extraordinary offer grew veiled through the language we adopted to explain Christian faith. Language tends to define, and sometimes limit, expectations. Currently, the common way to describe the essence of Christian experience in most circles would be along the lines of, "have faith in Christ." A good thing to have, faith is, but the phrase carries connotations. You can have faith without having much personal experience; you can hold to a certain religious faith and not actually know God yourself. (I've met many of these dear souls.) I have faith in my surgeon, but I don't know him at all. We certainly don't share our life together. I'm grateful for his help, but we aren't anything like best friends.

Evangelical teachers try to rectify this problem when they say things like, "Christianity is not a religion, it's a relationship." Which is closer to the truth. But union, oneness, integrated being—that is something else altogether.

I've been repeating as we go along that your soul is the vessel God fills. A basin is a receptacle: empty in itself, but it can be filled and was made to be filled. The water *inhabits* the fountain, which is a much closer metaphor. But the forest might be an even better picture; your being is porous like wood, not solid like marble. Your very being is made to be saturated with the being of God. You can have faith in God from a distance; you can have a "relationship" with Christ, but not be intimate. You can even find an intimacy with Christ, or your Father, or the Holy Spirit, and not be inhabited, interwoven, saturated.

Press your palms and fingers flat together like someone praying. Your left palm represents God, and your right palm you. This expression, I would say, is an expression of genuine intimacy. You and God are close. Now, while your palms remain pressed together, fold your fingers downward, so that the fingers of both hands become intertwined. This is an expression of deeper union, where your being and God's become intertwined. This entwining, this interlacing is what the hidden roots of the forest do. It might surprise some readers to hear me say this, but we are after much more than faith, even more than intimacy. We are after union, oneness—where our being and God's Being become intertwined. The substance of our life—our personality, our heart, our physicality, all of our experience—is filled over time to saturation with the substance of God's life.

1. In John 15, Jesus says our lives can become one shared existence with the Son of God, through whom all things were created, who sustains this glorious world. Do you think most believers understand or embrace this invitation? Why or why not?

2. Then Jesus ups the ante in John 17 by praying we would experience the same kind of united life and being with him that he experienced with his Father. Do you think most believers understand or embrace this deeper invitation? Why or why not?

3. Believers can have faith without having much personal experience. They can hold to a certain religious faith and not actually know God. How have you grown from initial faith in God to pursuing union with God?

DAY FIVE: HEALING OUR UNION WITH GOD

So it's not enough that we talk about how wonderful union can be, that we should make it a priority. That can all remain theory. We need to look into what has damaged our union with God.

I realize this is a very poignant thing I'm raising, and I want to proceed tenderly. Do you know what's damaged your soul's union with God?

Suffering in all its forms will slowly erode union, if we're not careful. As will chronic disappointment. Satan will use your suffering, or the suffering of those you love, to introduce mistrust between you and the God you love. *You see,* he whispers, *you are on your own. God's not here for you. He didn't do a thing to help.* The suffering or disappointment alone is enough to make us pull back, like a sea anemone does when you touch it. But these insidious words poison the relationship, and our union withers. We still might hang onto belief, but as we've seen, belief is not the same as saturated union. Has your suffering caused you to pull away? If we name it, we are able to come back toward God. We can choose to open up again, and ask him to heal our hearts, heal our union.

So I've found it very important to ask God to heal my union with him on a fairly regular basis, certainly after I've gone through something that felt traumatizing. Knowing I have a role to play (the door opens from the inside), I will pray something like this:

Father, Jesus, Holy Spirit—I need you to heal our union. Heal our union, God. I give myself to you, to be one with you in everything. I pray for union and I pray for oneness. I present my entire being to you, to be one life with you. I invite your healing love and presence into the things that have hurt our union. [Be specific if you can: The loss of my daughter. The betrayal at work. My chronic back pain.] I invite your Spirit into the places where our union has been assaulted. Come and heal me here. Cleanse these places with your blood, dear Jesus. Let your blood wash all wounding, wash away evil, cleanse every form of trauma in me. Bring your love here. I invite the light of your presence to bring healing here. I pray your glory would heal our union. May the glory of God come into the harm and damage, and restore our union. I pray to be one heart and mind again, one life, one complete union. [I will linger a moment to see if the Holy Spirit wants to show me anything specific I need to pray.] Heal our union, God; restore and renew our union. I pray for a deeper union with you, a deeper and more complete oneness. Restore our union, in Jesus's name.

(By offering this prayer I don't mean to imply that our souls are healed of trauma in one simple pass. I have seen God do this a number of times, but we need to be gracious and allow that we might need to see a counselor or seek some healing prayer ministry. This prayer is offered as a beginning. In the day-to-day wearing down of our union with God, this will restore it. In cases of more severe harm, more help is recommended.)

Remember, God works gently. He doesn't answer trauma with a forceful response; he heals through gentleness. Sometimes it can feel dramatic, but maybe only 5 percent of the time. Most of the time the union of our soul with God is something that is very gentle and life-giving. Therefore, you have to be gentle and tuned-in to be aware of it. Cultivating the Pause, and the other practices in this book, will certainly allow you to be in places that deepen union.

Then we will become those happy trees announced in Psalm 1, whose roots dwell deep down in living water; whose leaves never, ever wither; whose life is blossoming abundance season through season.

1. Over the years, how has suffering or chronic disappointment damaged your soul's union with God? Naming it helps us come back toward God.

2. Do you ask God to heal your union with him on a fairly regular basis, especially after going through something traumatizing? Have you realized you play a role in deepening your relationship with God?

3. How has God used gentleness to bring healing to your soul? Have you perhaps been unaware of these times until now because you were looking for a more dramatic intervention from God?

RECOMMENDED READING

Before your group meets for the next session, we encourage you to read chapter 14, "The Simple Daily Things," of *Get Your Life Back*. That chapter will be the focus of session 6.

SESSION 6

THE SIMPLE
DAILY THINGS

"You must ruthlessly eliminate hurry from your life."

DALLAS WILLARD

WELCOME

t's 5:20 p.m. on a midwinter day. The sun has almost set, and only now do I realize that not once have I even looked up at the sky today. I don't know if it's been cloudy or sunny. I don't know if the geese have been flying or if there was a beautiful sunrise. We live every moment of our lives under this gorgeous blue canopy, the dome of a great cathedral, and how seldom we enjoy it. My soul has been "gloved" today, cocooned in the artificial world.

In fact, the only reason I came outside at all is because of the injury one of our horses incurred. It is our bay, and somehow he turned up with a serious injury to his left hip. We're not quite sure how; things take place out in the pasture beyond our understanding. They can step in a hole, or something can startle them and they jump sideways and damage a leg, in the same way it's easy for a human being to tear their knee up on a simple run. Maybe he got a whiff of lion. Now I have to come every day to where we stable them in the winter and give our bay some exercise, gently walking him around, getting him to use his muscles, keep him from going lame. It's a serious thing for a horse to go lame. Our vet thought we might have to "put him down," as the horrible expression goes. That would have been heartbreaking.

So you can bet I've come every day. At first this task was stressful, filled with worry and concern. One more thing I needed to do in an already busy week. I secretly resented it.

But as we've progressed through this book together, we've explored the healing power of beauty and nature. We've talked about the grace of pauses in our day, the kindness of transitions, our need to get outside. Right here, in what I thought was one more grievance upon an already burdened life, it turns out God had something redemptive in mind. Being forced to stop my day, come here and spend time with these horses, has been a *rescue*. Life picks up momentum like a car on downhill ice, and it's so easy to just go with it. The pace is addictive; it gives us a false sense of purpose while also relieving us of paying attention to the deeper things. God gently slowed things down for me.

I'm just standing here, letting the horses graze while I hold their halters. I'm not productive; I'm gloriously inefficient.

Only now do I notice the clouds doing the most beautiful rippled pattern all across the southern sky, like a white silk scarf blowing ever so gently in an ocean breeze but translucent, so the haze of blue comes through. A herd of deer are cautiously grazing out into the field; there's a beautiful buck among them, with a gorgeous rack of antlers. For the first time I notice that the day has a scent to it, a distinctly winter tang— that mix of dried grasses and moist cold. Icy air has a metallic taste to it, like wet aluminum. As I walk our horses along, I look down and notice the dried many-flowered asters at my feet, how they were coated in ice last night and now look like tiny crystal goblets. This evening they are serving up a communion my heart desperately needed but only realized once I got out here and settled down.

The living presence of a horse beside me, his massive warm flanks, the weather, the quiet beauty are causing me to awaken, and as I do I'm aware again of the presence of God right here with me. Part of me wants to say, "Where have you been all day?" But I know the real question is where did *I* go all day?

GETTING STARTED

To begin this final session, discuss the following:

1. How has God used something that felt like one more thing on your to-do list in a redemptive manner?
2. Being busy can give us a false sense of purpose—even as we neglect our own souls. How has God slowed you down recently? What was your initial reaction to this intrusion into your plans?
3. How can you be more intentional about seeing God in the everyday?

CORE SCRIPTURE

Invite someone to read aloud the following words from Matthew 6. Listen for fresh insight and share any new thoughts with the group through the questions that follow.

Give us today our daily bread.

—Matthew 6:11

1. In just six simple words, what is Jesus inviting us to do here?

2. How does it offer a new perspective about the worries we're carrying from yesterday and the fear we have for tomorrow?

3. Do you wrestle with a sense of failure or frustration that no matter how much of God you experienced one day, you need more the next day? Is asking for more of God a part of your daily practices?

VIDEO TEACHING

Watch the video segment for session 6. A summary is provided for your benefit as well as space to take additional notes.

Summary

- Life is not lived in the fantastic. God is waiting for us in the dailies.

- The culture keeps pressuring us to be amazing but if you want your soul back, you're going to have to find it in the dailies.

- Your soul will let you know how it's doing through positive and negative barometers that serve as signposts and indicators.

- The soul eventually won't cooperate if it's neglected. If you're not receiving union in life or some joy, your soul will let you know.

- At this time in history where humanity is in such bad shape, we can be a countercultural presence—modern-day desert fathers and mothers. But that requires us to first care for our own souls.

- The world that we're living in requires a life that is saturated with God and a soul that is well, strong, and resilient.

- To get your life back, you'll need to do as Paul encourages in Philippians 4:9—just keep putting into practice the things you've seen and heard that are helpful to the soul and bring you more of God.

Notes

GROUP DISCUSSION

Take a few minutes to go through the following questions with your group.

1. Can you give an example of how you've looked for God in the amazing and missed him in the dailies?

2. Do you put pressure on yourself to be amazing—or think God was expecting "amazing" from you? Rest assured, God is nowhere in the pressure to be amazing. Can you release those false beliefs now?

3. How can you be more intentional about seeing God and pursuing soul care in the everyday?

4. What's an example of a negative barometer this week that tipped you off your soul was in need of care?

5. What's an example of a positive barometer this week that let you know your soul was doing well?

6. We often want to ask God, "Where have you been all day?" How does it shift our posture to ask instead, "Where did I go all day?"

CLOSING PRAYER

Wrap up your time together with prayer. Remember, prayer is simply talking to God. Here are a few ideas of what you could pray about based on the topics of this sixth session:

- Pray that God reveal himself to you in the dailies of life.
- Ask God to release you from the false burden of needing to be awesome.
- Seek his guidance on what the positive and negative parameters are for your soul.
- Express your desire to God to have more time for beauty.
- Tell God who he is and what you love about him.

GIVING IT A TRY

So the very simple question in this final session is this: What practices will you do, on a daily and weekly basis, to find God and receive more of him?

Today's invitation involves a piece of advice and a blessing.

First the advice. It comes from the apostle Paul, who lovingly and tenderly offered this to his dear sons and daughters in the faith:

> *Keep putting into practice all you learned and received from me—everything you heard from me and saw me doing. Then the God of peace will be with you* (Philippians 4:9, NLT).

There is such kindness in this encouragement. *Keep* putting into practice. It's not about perfection; it's not about being amazing. God is nowhere in the pressure to be amazing. He's waiting in the simple dailies. Just keep putting into practice the things that heal your soul and bring you more of Jesus. Then the God of peace will be with you. You'll no longer be sipping God from teaspoons; you'll learn to drink deeply from the tangible, nourishing, life-giving presence of the eternal God—Father, Son, and Holy Spirit—the fountain of living waters.

And now the blessing. It comes from Isaac of Stella.

May the Son of God, who is already formed in you, grow in you, so that for you he will become immeasurable, and that in you he will become laughter, exultation, the fullness of joy which no one can take from you.

FINAL PERSONAL STUDY

In this section, you can further explore the material we've covered this week. If you haven't already done so, we encourage you to read chapter 14, "The Simple Daily Things," of *Get Your Life Back* at this time. Each day offers a short reading from the book—along with reflection questions designed to take you deeper into the themes of this week's study. Journal or just jot a few thoughts after each question. The goal of these questions is for your personal growth and private reflection.

DAY ONE: POSITIVE AND NEGATIVE BAROMETERS

Life out there in the mad world remains what it is, spinning into greater frenzy, so we all need a quiver of gentle reminders—signs, symptoms, barometers—that let us know if we're living a sane life, healing the vessel God fills, creating opportunities for him to fill us. This world demands a life saturated with God, and this world is the perfect storm to prevent our souls from having it. We must shepherd our heart and soul with kindness and compassion so that the springs of life may flow freely, up through the fountain of our being (Proverbs 4:23).

I know I've been sucked back into the madness when I flinch at a request for any kind of help: the text of a friend asking for my time, the email seeking some counsel. Or when Stasi shares the report of friends in crisis and everything in me wants to pull away rather than move toward them. Or when I don't even want to look at email, because I know there are demands waiting for me there. The flinch, wince, long hesitation, unhappy sigh; the avoidance, the inability to enter in—these are symptoms that we're running on fumes again.

Our capacity for relationship is such a wonderful gauge. We are created in the image of a profoundly relational God, created for relationship. Am I available for relationship? Not with everyone all the time of course—I'm not meaning the entire social network with no boundaries whatsoever, not 24/7 access. I'm talking about the people in my life: loved ones, colleagues, neighbors out walking their dogs. If I've lost the capacity for, and the *enjoyment* of relationship, I know things are deeply off in my soul.

Sugar and caffeine are always warning signs. Have I moved from enjoying them to needing them, relying on them to get me through the rest of my day? What about a simple pause? Even though I wrote the book, the One Minute Pause can be so disruptive on some days, even irritating. Yikes. If I'm hassled by a sixty-second pause, I'm deep down the drainpipe.

But there are positive barometers, too, wonderful things; these are so much better to watch. Have I seen my horses? Was I able to pay attention to what Stasi was saying this morning?

Am I making room for beauty, nature, the act of simply loving God? Positive signs and reminders are better for us to watch, because these slip away before you begin to really sink in the mire. If I've reached the point that I don't want to play with my grandchildren, I'm not well. But way before that happens, I can tell how I'm doing if I'm neglecting the simple practices that bring me healing, solace, more of God.

1. What are the signs that let you know when you've been sucked back into the madness of this crazy world?

2. What are your top three positive barometers for how your soul is doing—and what is it specifically about these things that reveal your soul is thriving?

3. What are your top three negative barometers for how your soul is doing—and what is it specifically about these things that reveal how your soul is struggling?

DAY TWO: YOUR SANCTUARY "SPACE"

My daily walk is a good benchmark because it's simple, accessible, and tells me whether or not I'm living realistically. I'm not talking about hours wandering through the enchanted forest (though I love that); I'm talking about a twenty-minute walk in the evening. How affirming to see this included in a list of "The Daily Routines of Geniuses," published in *Harvard Business Review*. The author compared the schedules and lifestyles of "161 painters, writers, and composers, as well as philosophers, scientists, and other exceptional thinkers" and discovered they all shared some things in common:

- A workspace with minimal distractions
- A daily walk (many would write in the morning, stop for lunch and a stroll, spend an hour or two answering letters, and knock off work by two or three in the afternoon)
- A clear dividing line between important work and busywork
- Limited social lives[24]

I know, I know, it sounds idyllic—something from a bygone era. Maybe. You can't get out for a walk? You can't cut back your social life, which in this culture means cutting down your social media and texting? Both are very doable. I love the idea of making your home or apartment a place that feels restorative to your soul. You want your "space," whatever it is, to be your sanctuary and haven, even if your neighbor loves his leaf blower.

Sometimes the places we go for soul care need a little care. When I walked into my home office to work on this book, I was struck by the fact that the visual experience before me was exactly the same as it has been for sixteen years. Same things on my desk, same view out the window, same artwork on the walls. It had gone stale long ago; I'd just gotten used to it. I needed freshness. I needed to clear out the accumulated clutter. I needed a space that corresponded to the very things I'm writing about, a space my soul felt good to be in. So I spent a few days redoing my office: moving furniture, returning to the bookcases the many volumes that had wound up stacked on the floor, shuffling off to the garage various gear that could better be stored there. Mostly what I did was simplify. I made it a space that felt quieting to walk into.

1. What is your preferred sanctuary "space"? What makes it restorative to your soul?

2. How many of the four traits shared by the 161 exceptional thinkers (from "The Daily Routines of Geniuses" article) are currently part of your lifestyle? Which new practice would you like to incorporate most—and what would it take to do so?

3. Throughout this study, we've focused on ways to unclutter your soul. How might you simplify or unclutter your home and workspace to make them more of a haven?

DAY THREE: YOUR ABILITY TO ENJOY

We know now that the internet is messing with our brains, making it nearly impossible to pay attention to anything for more than a flit and a flicker. When I read Nicholas Carr's experience, I winced in seeing my own:

> I began to notice that the Net was exerting a much stronger and broader influence over me than my old stand-alone PC ever had. It wasn't just that I was spending so much time staring into a computer screen. It wasn't just that so many of my habits and routines were changing as I became more accustomed to and dependent on the sites and services of the Net. The very way my brain worked seemed to be changing. It was then that I began worrying about my inability to pay attention to one thing for more than a couple of minutes. At first I figured the problem was a symptom of middle-age mind rot. But my brain, I realized, wasn't just drifting. It was hungry.

It was demanding to be fed the way the Net fed it—
and the more it was fed, the hungrier it became.
Even when I was away from my computer, I yearned
to check email, click links, do some Googling. I
wanted to be *connected* . . . the Internet, I sensed, was
turning me into something like a high-speed data
processing machine. . .

I missed my old brain.[25]

When I read that, I thought, *I miss my* soul. The world is
changing our habits and routines; we need to push back.
So enjoying a book or magazine has become an act of self-
defense. As is time to enjoy making, and lingering, over
dinner. Several times a week. Honestly, simply the ability to
enjoy *anything* is a good sign to watch for.

Along with this I would add "the ability to hope and
dream." Are you looking forward to your future? What are
you dreaming about these days? Or are you hunkered down,
braced against the world, just getting by? Let that test be a
sign to you.

1. Nicholas Carr makes this comment about the effect of
   the internet and modern technology: "The very way my
   brain worked seemed to be changing." Do you sense
   technology has caused a change in your attention span
   or focus? If so, how?

2. On a deeper level, how do you feel the modern world is changing our habits and routines in unhealthy ways?

3. The ability to enjoy anything is what's often lost as the pace of life accelerates. What brings you joy regularly? What is a big dream you have for your future?

DAY FOUR: RECEIVING GOD'S GIFTS

I saw a moose coming over the pass a few weeks ago; she had run across the road and was just disappearing into the woods when I caught my glimpse. These are the pennies from heaven Annie Dillard talks about:

> Unwrapped gifts and free surprises. The world is fairly strewn and studded with pennies cast broadside from a generous hand. . . . If you crouch motionless on a bank to see a tremulous ripple thrill on the water and are rewarded by the sight of a musk-rat kit paddling from its den, will you count that

sight a chip of copper only, and go on your rueful way? It is dire poverty indeed when a man is so malnourished and fatigued that he won't stoop to pick up a penny.[26]

Or those hundred-dollar gifts of beauty God keeps leaving for us. Remember—stop and receive these gifts: *Thank you for this beauty, Father. I receive it into my soul. I receive this gift and through it your love, your goodness, your life.*

What will your barometers be? The negative ones are obvious: when you find yourself hating your political opponents, framing angry Facebook replies in your mind, wanting to run bad drivers off the road. But what's on the positive side? Is it listening to music in the evening? If so you know that when you haven't for several weeks, things are amiss.

We have a lot of dog walkers in our neighborhood, mostly out in the mornings and evenings. I've been watching this one fellow who has an odd-looking, mid-sized dog that doesn't fit any breed I'm familiar with; he looks like a loaf of bread. Cute, but he seems reluctant to participate in the walking ritual. Every time I see them, the owner is out front, arm and leash fully extended behind him. Coming along behind, moseying, not forlorn but just kind of at his own pace, is this little mutt. The owner is clearly trying to get some exercise ("get a workout in," as the saying goes, because it is something to be jammed into a frenzied life). His dog on the other hand is simply out to be out, to enjoy the world. Today the mutt had rolled over on his back on the sidewalk, paws up in the air in playful protest, while the owner was out front, arm and leash fully extended, tugging to get his companion moving. It made me laugh.

And then I realized—that's my soul; that's me and my soul. I'm trying to get my soul to come along in a way of life it just doesn't want to cooperate with. Pay attention: if it feels like you're dragging your soul along behind you, take notice. Maybe you're asking it to work at the speed of advanced technology; maybe it means you're asking it to move too quickly through the myriad challenges of your life, with no transition. It might just need to lie on its back and put its paws in the air for a few minutes.

1. What "pennies from heaven" has God placed in your life recently?

2. When you come across these "unwrapped gifts and free surprises," how good are you at stopping to fully receive them? Explain.

3. Do you sometimes feel like you're dragging your soul behind you? Can you name what you tend to be doing—or what's happening to you—when that's the case?

DAY FIVE: MORE OF GOD!

Now, two little qualifications, or clarifications, to the use of barometers.

First, something is going to happen to you, may already be happening, which could really throw you for a loop without some interpretation. Augustine described the whole life of the Christian as a holy longing. Your heart is going to grow for the kingdom, more and more as you mature, which allows us to receive more and more of God and *enjoy* so much more of the life he's giving. But this can be very disorienting if you don't understand what's taking place within you. Just as you reach a place where you feel satisfied, it seems you need more. That's because your soul is expanding, which is a very good thing.

Some of the old habits, even the old comforts, just won't work anymore; some of your old relationships won't either, nor will certain religious associations. You no longer fit. We can think there's something wrong with us, when what's happening is that we are being healed toward heaven, toward Eden. As our soul is restored, it will fit less and less into the madness of this world and this hour, which, sadly, has infected Christianity quite deeply. No judgments, no need to make a scene. But you're not a moral failure because you don't fit; you're being healed. Time to move on.

The second caution comes to us through the Old Testament story of manna. The entire nation of Israel is ransomed from Egypt "with a strong hand and powerful arm, with overwhelming terror, and with miraculous signs and wonders" (Deuteronomy 26:8, NLT). Stepping through the sundered waters of the Red Sea, the people find themselves in a roundabout trek, zigzagging across the arid desert of the Sinai Peninsula (with no annual rainfall to speak of). Masses of people wandering barren wasteland are going to die for lack of food and water in a matter of weeks, maybe days. Forty years is out of the question. So God provides his people with the bread of angels every morning. They couldn't store it, they couldn't hoard it. They had to go out each morning and gather it. And it was always there, delivered silently, gently.

Now, why did God give us this unforgettable parable?

Because no matter how much of God we've finally been able to partake of, the surprising "aha" is that we need it again tomorrow. I always thought that, for some reason, I could get to a place where I was tapped into God in such a way I didn't run out. But we need to sleep again every night; we need to drink water every day; we need to breathe again every single moment. Your life is a beautifully dependent existence, like the tree and the forest. You're not failing because you need God again tomorrow. You're not a spiritual disaster because you need so much more of him. This is the nature of things. We simply come and ask. "Give us today our daily bread" (Matthew 6:11).

We practice those things that bring us more of God.

1. Have you experienced what Augustine refers to as "holy longing"—where just as you reach a place that you feel satisfied, it seems you need more? Have you realized that's actually a good thing because it means your soul is expanding?

2. As your soul is restored, it will fit less and less into the madness of this world. How does it feel to realize some of your prior habits, comforts, relationships, and even religious associations won't fit anymore?

3. No matter how much of God you're able to partake of, the surprising "aha" is that you'll need it again tomorrow. Do you view your life as a beautifully dependent existence? How might doing so take the pressure off and bring life to your soul?

LEADER'S GUIDE

Thank you for your willingness to lead your group through *Get Your Life Back: Everyday Practices for a World Gone Mad.* The rewards of leading are different from the rewards of participating, and we hope you find your own walk with Jesus deepened by this experience. This leader's guide will give you some tips on how to prepare for your time together and facilitate a meaningful experience for your group members.

WHAT DOES IT TAKE TO LEAD THIS STUDY?

Get together and watch God show up. Seriously, that's the basics of how a small group works. Gather several people together who have a hunger for God, want to learn how to get their lives back, and are willing to be open and honest with God and themselves. The Lord will honor this every time and show up in the group. You don't have to be a pastor, priest, theologian, or counselor to lead a group through this study. Just invite people over, watch the video, and talk about it. All you need is a willing heart, a little courage, and God will do the rest. Really.

HOW THIS STUDY WORKS

As the group leader, you will want to make sure everyone in your group has a copy of this study guide. (The group members will also want to have a copy of the *Get Your Life Back* book if they are doing the recommended readings for each session.) It works best if you can get the guides (and books) to your group *before* the first meeting. That way, everyone can read the material in the book ahead of time and be prepared to watch the first video session together.

This series is presented in six video sessions, with each session being approximately fifteen to twenty minutes in length. Each week, you will meet together to watch the video and discuss the session. This series can also be used in classroom settings, such as Sunday school classes, though you may need to modify the discussion time depending on the size of the class. You could even use the video as sessions for a special prayer retreat.

Basically, each week you will: (1) discuss the opening Getting Started and Core Scripture questions, (2) watch the video sessions, (3) talk about it, and then (4) reflect on what you have learned by completing the between-sessions activities. That's it!

A FEW TIPS FOR LEADING A GROUP

The setting really matters. If you can choose to meet in a living room over a conference room in a church, do it. Pick an environment that's conducive to people relaxing and getting real. Remember the enemy likes to distract us when it comes to seeking God, so do what you can to remove these obstacles from your group (silence cell phones, limit background noise, no texting). Set the chairs or couches in a circle to prevent having a "classroom" feel.

Have some refreshments! Coffee and water will do; cookies and snacks are even better. People tend to be nervous when they join a new group, so if you can give them something to hold onto (like a warm mug of coffee), they will relax a lot more. It's human nature.

Good equipment is important. Meet where you can watch the video sessions on a screen big enough for everyone to see and enjoy. Get or borrow the best gear you can. Also, be sure to test your media equipment ahead of time to make sure everything is in working condition. This way, if something isn't working, you can fix it or make other arrangements before the meeting begins. (You'll be amazed at how the enemy will try to mess things up for you!)

Be honest. Remember that your honesty will set the tone for your time together. Be willing to answer questions personally, as this will set the pace for the length of your group members' responses and will make others more comfortable in sharing.

Stick to the schedule. Strive to begin and end at the same time each week. The people in your group are busy, and if they can trust you to be a good steward of their time, they will be more willing to come back each week. Of course, you want to be open to the work God is doing, and at times you may want to *linger* in prayer or discussion. Remember the clock serves *you;* your group doesn't serve the clock. But work to respect the group's time, especially when it comes to limiting the discussion times.

Don't be afraid of silence or emotion. Welcome awkward moments. The material presented during this study will challenge the group members to reconsider some of their beliefs and compel them to make the necessary changes in their lives. Don't be afraid to ease into the material with the group.

Don't dominate the conversation. Even though you are the leader, you are also a member of this small group. So don't steamroll over others in an attempt to lead—and don't let anyone else in the group do so either.

Prepare for your meeting. Watch the video for the meeting ahead of time. Although it may feel a bit like cheating because you'll know what's coming, you will be better prepared for what the session might stir in the hearts of your group members. Also be sure to review the material in this guide and spend some time in prayer. In fact, the *most important* thing you can do is simply pray ahead of time each week:

> *Lord Jesus, come and rule this time. Let your Spirit fill this place. Bring your kingdom here. Take us right to the things we really need to talk about and rescue us from every distraction. Show us the heart of the Father. Meet each person here. Give us your grace and love for one another. In your name I pray.*

Make sure your group members are prepared. Before the first meeting, secure enough copies of the study guide for each member. Have these ready and on hand for the first meeting, or make sure the participants have purchased them. Send out a reminder email or a text a couple of days before the meeting to make sure folks don't forget about it.

AS YOU GATHER

You will find the following counsel to be especially helpful when you meet for the first time as a group. I offer these comments in the spirit of "here is what I would do if I were leading a group through this study."

First, as the group gathers, start your time with introductions if people don't know each other. Begin with yourself and share your name, how long you've been a follower of Christ, if you have a spouse and/or children, and what you want to learn most from this study on getting your life back. Going first will put the group more at ease.

After each person has introduced himself or herself, go through the Getting Started and Core Scripture sections as you have time. Then jump right into watching the video session, as this will help get things started on a strong note. In the following weeks, you may want to start by allowing folks to catch up a little with some "how are you?" kind of banter. Too much of this burns up your meeting time, but you have to allow some room for it because it helps build relationships among the group members.

Note that each group will have its own personality and dynamics. Typically, people will hold back the first week or two until they feel the group is "safe." Then they will begin to share. Again, don't let it throw you if your group seems a bit awkward at first. Of course, some people *never* want to talk, so you'll need to coax them out as time goes on. But let it go the first week.

INSIGHT FOR DISCUSSION

If the group members are in any way open to talking about their lives as it relates to this material, you will likely *not* have enough time for every question suggested in this study guide. That's okay! Pick the questions ahead of time that you know you definitely want to cover, just in case you end up only having time to discuss a few of them.

You set the tone for the group. Your honesty and vulnerability during discussion times will tell them what they can share. How *long* you talk will give them an example of how long they should respond. So give some thought to what stories or insights from your own work in the study guide you want to highlight.

WARNING: The greatest temptation for small group leaders is to add to the video teaching with a little "teaching session" of their own. This is unhelpful for three reasons:

1. The discussion time will be the richest time during your meeting. The video sessions have been intentionally kept short so you can have plenty of time for discussion. If you add to the teaching, you sacrifice this precious time.

2. You don't want your group members *teaching*, *lecturing*, or *correcting* one another. The group

members are all at different places in their spiritual journey. If you set a tone by teaching, the group will feel like they have the freedom to teach one another. That can be disastrous for group dynamics.

3. The participants will be watching the video teachings during your group time and exploring the topics covered in more detail by completing the between-sessions activities. They don't need more content! What they want is a chance to talk and process their own lives in light of all they have taken in.

A STRONG CLOSE

Some of the best learning times will take place after the group time as God brings new insights to the participants during the week. Encourage group members to write down any questions they have as they work through the between-sessions exercises. Make sure they know you are available for them as they explore what God has to say about reclaiming their lives from the constant distractions of this world. Finally, make sure you close your time by praying together—either by following the suggested prompts or coming up with your own closing prayers. Ask two or three people to pray, inviting God to fill your group and lead each person during this study.

Thank you again for taking the time to lead your group. May God reward your efforts and dedication and make your time together in *Get Your Life Back* fruitful for his kingdom.

ENDNOTES

1. J. R. R. Tolkien, *The Fellowship of the Ring* (New York: Ballantine Books, 1954), p. 34.
2. Thomas Merton, *The Wisdom of the Desert* (New York: New Directions, 1960), p. 3.
3. St. Augustine, "Expositions on the Book of Psalms," in *A Library of Fathers of the Holy Catholic Church* (London: F. & J. Rivington, 1857), p. 167.
4. Nicholas Carr, *The Shallows: What the Internet Is Doing to Our Brains* (New York: W. W. Norton, 2011), pp. 5–9.
5. Carr, pp. 114–143.
6. Carr, pp. 220–222.
7. Seth Goden, "Mobile Blindness," Seth's Blog, March 21, 2018 https://seths.blog/2018/03/mobile-blindness.
8. Matthew B. Crawford, *The World Beyond Your Head: On Becoming an Individual in an Age of Distraction* (New York: Farrar, Straus & Giroux, 2016), p. ix.
9. Susan Weinschenk, "Why We're All Addicted to Texts, Twitter and Google," *Psychology Today*, September 11, 2012, http:// www.physchologytoday.com/ us/blog/brain-wise/201209/why-were-all-addicted-texts-twitter-google.
10. Asurion, "Tech-Tips," https://www.asurion.com/connect/tech-tips.
11. Robert M. Pirsig, *Zen and the Art of Motorcycle Maintenance: An Inquiry Into Values* (New York: HarperCollins, 2006), p. 4.
12. Scott Yorko, "The Science of Why You Love the Wilderness," *Backpacker*, June 14, 2017, https//www.backpacker.com/news-and-events/ science-of-why-you-love-the-wilderness.
13. Elaine Scarry, *On Beauty and Being Just* (Princeton, N.J.: Princeton University Press, 1999), 23–25.
14. Scarry, p. 50.
15. Scarry, p. 69.
16. Scarry, p. 47.
17. Scarry, p. 33.

18. Jake Miller, "Better by Design," *Harvard Medicine* (Spring 2019), http://hms.harvard.edu/magazine/assembled-care-better-design.
19. Society for Human Resource Management, "2016 Paid Leave in the Workplace," SHRM, October 6, 2016, https://www.shrm.org/hr-today/trends-and-forecasting/research-and-surveys/pages/2016-paid-leave-in-the-workplace.aspx.
20. Mark Twain, *Chapters from My Autobiography* (Oxford: Benediction Classics, 2011), 24.
21. Peter Wohlleben, *The Hidden Life of Trees: What They Feel, How They Communicate: Discoveries from a Secret World* (Munich: Ludvig Verlag, 2015), pp. 1–2.
22. Wohlleben, pp. 15, 18.
23. Wohlleben, pp. 8–10.
24. Sarah Green Carmichael, "The Daily Routines of Geniuses," *Harvard Business Review*, March 19, 2014, https://hbr.org/2014/03/the-daily-routines-of-geniuses.
25. Nicholas Carr, *The Shallows*, p. 16.
26. Annie Dillard, *Pilgrim at Tinker Creek* (New York: HarperCollins, 2009), p. 17.

Experience the One Minute Pause App on Your Phone Today

"I've developed an app to help you practice the Pause. It's the beginning of a new way of living. Your soul is going to thank you."

John

WWW.PAUSEAPP.COM

You've read *Get Your Life Back*—
so you know the importance of
regular soul care. For fresh weekly
encouragement, listen to John
Eldredge on the Ransomed Heart
podcast. The conversations,
stories, and teachings will
strengthen your heart.

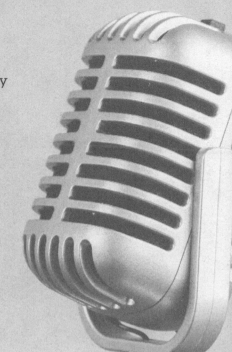

JOIN US FOR

John Eldredge's
Weekly Podcast

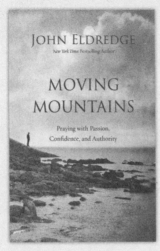
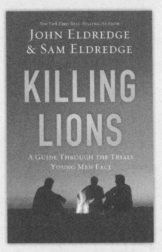
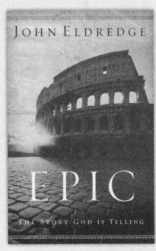
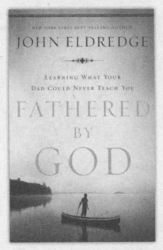

MORE RESOURCES FROM
RANSOMED HEART

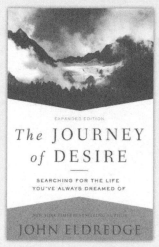

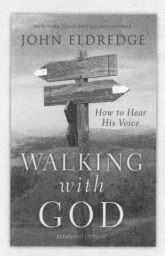

Study guide available

Video curriculum and
study guide available

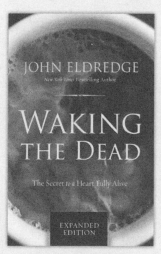

Study Guide available

Video curriculum and
study guide available

FOR MORE PROJECTS AND INFORMATION
VISIT US AT RANSOMEDHEART.COM

Read the Book That Inspired This Study

JOHN ELDREDGE
New York Times Bestselling Author

get your life back

EVERYDAY PRACTICES FOR A WORLD GONE MAD

CONGRATULATIONS ON PARTICIPATING IN THIS SIX-WEEK STUDY TO GET YOUR LIFE BACK.

The good news is...there is even more! The book *Get Your Life Back* includes additional chapters not featured in the video or study guide. To go deeper in this message and discover new practices for soul care, read *Get Your Life Back*.

www.johneldredge.com